V ORLEANS

Lithograph from the collection of Raymond Samuel

The NEW ORLEANS *Restaurant* COOKBOOK

The NEW ORLEANS *Restaurant* COOKBOOK

WRITTEN AND ILLUSTRATED BY

DEIRDRE STANFORTH

DOUBLEDAY & COMPANY,.INC.

GARDEN CITY, NEW YORK

PHOTOGRAPH CREDITS

New Orleans Chamber of Commerce: The French Quarter, pages 18–19
Leon Trice: Façade and Interior of Antoine's, pages 20, 23, 26
Commercial Kitchen and Dining Room Magazine: Antoine's Kitchen, page 28
Vieux Carré Survey: Galatoire's, page 48
Bernadas-Weiss: Dunbar's Exterior, page 54
Ronald Montelepre: Dunbar's Dining Room and Parlor, pages 56, 58
Frank Lotz Miller: Commander's Exterior Patio and Bar, pages 68, 71, 74
V. Thomas Kersh: Commander's Dining Room with Chandelier, page 76
James Ricau: Plantation Mansion, pages 90–91

Library of Congress Catalog Card Number 67–19107

Printed in the United States of America

9 8 7 6 5 4 3

CONTENTS

ILLUSTRATIONS

PHOTOGRAPHS

DRAWINGS

ACKNOWLEDGMENTS

Rather than dedicate this book to any one person, I would like to thank all those who helped make it possible. Most essential was the assistance of the restaurant owners. I am everlastingly grateful for their cooperation and patient forbearance through endless interviews, questions, and nagging for recipes. I am only too well aware of the interruptions I caused in their busy schedules—indeed, Albert Aschaffenburg, whose initial enthusiasm assisted in the birth of this project, ended by referring to it affectionately as "that damn book"! My sincere and heartfelt thanks to all of them—I only hope I have done them justice.

I am indebted also to those hard-working behind-the-scenes assistants not mentioned in the following chapters: Magdelene Willoz of Arnaud's, Jewel Tyler of the Pontchartrain, and Euphemie Blanc of Brennan's.

Chefs Nathaniel (Burt) Burton, Irving Jones, and James Evans contributed a great deal—and I shall never forget my conferences with them in kitchens, over the proverbial hot stove, and even inside refrigerators.

Others I should like to thank include Raymond Samuel—for allowing me to reproduce his unique and marvelous old print of Jackson Square, as well as for his valuable suggestions and the useful research material in articles and booklets he has written; John Chase, for his delightful reminiscences about the Sazerac Bar; Leonard Huber, who gave me access to his remarkable collection of New Orleans prints; Margaret Ruckert, who steered me to the best sources of research in the New Orleans Public Library; Bette Moore; and my old friend Glen Douthit of the New Orleans Tourist Commission.

Perhaps I owe the largest debt of gratitude to Tess Crager of the Basement Bookshop and the Robert L. Crager Publishing Company—my mother. This book was her idea. And my undertaking to write it is (for better or worse) surely her responsibility. Although I consider art my career, it is impossible to live in her orbit without becoming involved in books. Her literary influence in general and doing *Brennan's New Orleans Cookbook* for her in particular were essential experience in preparation for this work. She is also an invaluable source of information and reminiscences about her beloved New Orleans, and it helped not a little with the New Orleans restaurant owners that I was her daughter.

My sincere appreciation and obeisances not only to my editor at Doubleday, Clara Claasen, but to my editor at home, Jim Stanforth. I am utterly dependent on his keen critical sense, his objective eye, and his rapier-sharp blue pencil. It is entirely my fault that he was diverted to another profession from the book-publishing world into which we both were born, so the very least I can do is to say quite truthfully that this book is his as well as mine.

DEIRDRE STANFORTH

Introduction

New Orleans is the most food-conscious community in America; in fact, it may well be the only city outside of France where eating is a major love affair of the population.

Undoubtedly the fact that New Orleans began as a French possession had a great deal to do with the development of this gourmania, but the years that the city lived under Spanish domination had their influence, too.

No other cuisine has been born of so many nationalities: a combination of spicy Spanish seasoning, Italian oils, the culinary art of the French provinces, of Paris and Marseilles, and the elegant artistry of aristocratic refugees from the French Revolution—mixed with the native American Indian influence, and all stirred together with the natural skill of the Negro. The resulting cuisine is called Creole.*

A vital element in the evolution of the Creole cuisine was the accessibility of so many ingredients. The best produce came down the river to the mouth of the Mississippi from all of North America and up through the Gulf from South America and Mexico. Seafood abounded in neighboring lakes and rivers and the woods were full of game. Indian wild herbs and vegetables played an important part in the development of Creole cooking: mirlitons, plantains, yams, okra, and particularly filé powder, made by the Choctaws from the tender young leaves of the Sassafras,** an essential ingredient of gumbo.

In the *Historical Sketch Book and Guide to New Orleans and Environs* by William H. Coleman, published in 1885, gumbo is beautifully described as follows: "The great dish of New Orleans, and

* A Creole is anyone born in the colonies of European ancestry, French or Spanish or both.

** The filé leaves, as well as all other kinds of produce, were hawked in the streets. Well into the first half of the twentieth century the colorful cries of the street vendors still rang through the city—with "straw-berrieees," "black-berrieees," "figs," "river swimp" and "*calas tout chaud*." There was even a man who drove a horse-drawn wagon, blowing a bugle to announce his delicious hot waffles sprinkled with powdered sugar.

which it claims the honor of having invented, is the GUMBO. There is no dish which at the same time so tickles the palate, satisfies the appetite, furnishes the body with nutriment sufficient to carry on the physical requirements, and costs so little as a Creole gumbo. It is a dinner in itself, being soup, *pièce de résistance, entremet* and vegetable in one. Healthy, not heating to the stomach and easy of digestion, it should grace every table."

Admiring newspaper and magazine articles by surprised and pleased visitors of that day exclaimed over the distinctive gumbos of oyster, crab, shrimp, and chicken, not complete without tomato, okra, and filé—delicate bisques, hearty bean soups, four different kinds of bread, oysters baked on the half shell—Bourguignonne and Rockefeller, and shrimp and crabs served in dozens of different ways.

A fascinating custom that manifested itself in New Orleans in 1837 was the free lunch. Gentlemen doing business in the French portion of the city could not get home for lunch and did not want to pay restaurant prices for "a mere plate of soup and a sandwich. To gratify this large class and secure their custom" the first-class hotel barrooms (beginning with the bar in the old St. Louis Hotel) inaugurated free lunches. They were served on a narrow table cloth running the whole length of the counter and covering half of it. As the customer's drink was set before him, he was served soup, beef or ham, potatoes, meat pie, or oyster patties. The bill of fare increased as the custom became more and more popular. The restaurants, finding it injurious to their business, tried to put a stop to it—without success.

As for the restaurants, according to the *New Orleans Guide* of 1885 by James Zacharie, they all had rooms upstairs where they took in boarders by month or week, and two meals were furnished (this was true of the early establishments of Antoine's and Arnaud's). And from the same book: "Ladies do not dine generally in the open saloon of the restaurants except during the Carnival week. Rooms are attached to all restaurants where ladies may dine with or without escorts."

Restaurants were kept by Frenchmen and in the French style. Dishes were a mixture of French and Creole cooking, "which is highly seasoned and much appreciated by 'bon vivants.'" Moreau's, at 128 Canal Street, was considered the leading and best restaurant at that time. Enormously popular, though open only for breakfast, was the legendary and colorful Begué's. Founded in 1863 as a coffeehouse (of which there were a great many at that time) its proprietor was a Creole, Louis Dutrey. Located across the street from the French Market, Dutrey's Coffee House lured the butchers for their "second breakfast" with the cooking of his German wife, Elisabeth Kettenring. The butchers followed the French custom of an early cup of coffee or glass of wine with a chunk of French bread before going to work at daybreak. When business slacked off at 11 A.M. they had their second breakfast.

After Dutrey's death, his widow married Hypolite Begué, one of the French butchers who had been a regular customer. In 1880 the coffeehouse changed its name to Begué's, and by 1884 its fame had spread outside the French Market. Soon it became the custom for Creole dandies and aristocrats to climb the narrow stairs to the butcher's coffeehouse across from the French Market for Sunday morning breakfast, beginning at 11 A.M. and never ending until 3 P.M. One early guidebook has this listing: "Begué's, 823 Decatur Street, is a great place for Bohemian breakfasts for ladies and gentlemen, at 11:00 o'clock ($1.00 including wine). As there is always a demand for seats they should be reserved by telephone."

Madame Begué presided behind a desk as she supervised the serving of crawfish, snails, or tripe, omelets, halved tomatoes with parsley, beefsteak, cheese, apples, coffee, and brandy. (Which rather makes Brennan's breakfasts sound like diet repasts.) Judging from old photographs, Begué's was quaint but crude, which just goes to prove that New Orleanians don't care where they eat as long as the food is good. And "good" must be a masterpiece of understatement in describing the fare at Madame Begué's. There was even a *Madame Begué's Creole Cookbook,* which is unfortunately long since out of print. After Madame Begué died, Hypolite carried on the business with his second wife, but when he died in 1917, Begué's died with him, and the building now houses Tujaque's, run by John Castet, who worked for Hypolite. Tujaque's is still there, featuring hearty, inexpensive meals of enormous quantity. There is no menu and no choice—the food just arrives, course after endless course.

Another restaurant from the same era and with the same type of food as Tujaque's is Maylie's—one of the oldest, after Antoine's and Galatoire's. However, it now calls itself a private club.

The restaurants of New Orleans deserve their extraordinary reputation. They are magnificent. Many common bonds unite them all—a rather fascinating phenomenon is that almost all of them are family businesses. Unlike some of the great restaurants of New York that are run by managers representing huge chains that own them, the New Orleans restaurants in this book are not only owner-operated by passionately interested people who are always on the scene supervising the quality of food and service, but many of them involve entire families in the business, passing it down as a proud legacy from one generation to the next.

New Orleans, while certainly one of the nation's larger cities (and growing at a fantastic rate), is at the same time a very provincial one, with fierce civic pride. Perhaps this explains the extraordinary camaraderie among the restaurant owners. Far from behaving like competitors, they are exceedingly friendly and loyal to one another. You will never hear one of them criticize another. As one explained, since New Orleans is so famous for its restaurants, any tourist expects to sample several of them—so it is only logical to recommend the others to him. Not only that, but there is a strong feeling that what is good for New Orleans as a whole benefits each one of them in particular. A good example of this community spirit was displayed during a strike that threatened to close down Arnaud's. On a moment's notice, all the other leading restaurant owners rallied round, replacing the missing employees, with Ernest Masson presiding over the kitchen as chef, Brennans and Morans as captains and cashiers, etc.

You will also find in delving into their backgrounds that there is considerable interweaving of past relationships—of Count Arnaud with Owen Brennan; of Albert Dubos, founder of Masson's, with the Alciatores, founders of Antoine's; and so on. Arnaud is said to have needled Brennan into starting his restaurant, and Roy Alciatore enjoyed teasing Arnaud about the magazine that recommended the Shrimp Arnaud at Antoine's.

It is worth noting before eating or cooking in the New Orleans style that often familiar culinary nomenclature has a different meaning in the Crescent City. Remoulade sauce in New Orleans is entirely unrecognizable from the classic French recipe from which it was derived. Originally a mayonnaise lightly flavored with pickles, parsley, and herbs, in New Orleans it has become a fiery sauce with mayonnaise only a very minor ingredient. Each restaurant has its own variation (Arnaud's being most famous—but they will only reveal the ingredients without quantities, since it is patented and sold in bottles), and they all differ substantially. Bordelaise sauce means one thing in France and quite another in New Orleans. New Orleanians even have their own lexicon of the kitchen, using "bell pepper" for green pepper, preferring "shallots" to green onions or scallions, and "breakfast cream" rather than light cream. Then of course there is the "roux," the basis of Creole sauces, for which the flour is stirred into the fat and the liquid added at the beginning of the dish, instead of being used as a thickening agent at the end. New Orleans shares the taste of all tropical climes for hot food, so if you aspire to reproduce New Orleans cuisine, when it says "season to taste," it means *spicy*.

With their common heritage in the Creole cuisine, there is bound to be duplication of dishes among the restaurants—each has its gumbo, its turtle soup, its crawfish bisque. It would be pointless to give eight recipes for each of these dishes, so with certain exceptions —the remoulade sauce, for one—in which variations make repetition worthwhile, one recipe has been chosen as representative. When a restaurant is known for certain specialties, that restaurant's recipe is featured, unless it is a secret—as is true of Antoine's Oysters Rockefeller and Dunbar's Oysters and Artichoke. In a few cases a recipe mentioned in the text does not appear in the recipe section. Where this occurs, it is due to the policy of family secrecy rather than oversight or deliberate omission.

Dishes will be listed in this book as appetizers or entrees as they are on the menus of the restaurants of their origin, but in many cases an appetizer, or a soup such as gumbo, makes an excellent entree especially for luncheons.

To some the choice of New Orleans' leading restaurants as featured in this book may seem arbitrary or unfair. This selection was arrived at from the objective vantage point of a native who has spent half her life in New Orleans and half in New York. After careful consideration and discussion with local cognoscenti, these eight were chosen. Apologies to those who disagree—and *bon appétit* to all!

RESTAURANTS

FOLLOWING PAGES: *New Orleans – City of Restaurants*

Façade of Antoine's

Antoine's

Antoine's is probably the world's most famous restaurant. Founded in 1840 by Antoine Alciatore, it is today operated at its original location by his descendants, and has never for one day of its more than century-old existence been without an Alciatore in charge to maintain its high standards for exquisite cuisine.

Behind the typical French Quarter façade is a deliberately plain dining room with white-tiled floor, hatracks, Victorian brass chandeliers, and the original early gas mantles, which provide the only heat in winter. The very large banquet hall adjoining has its red walls covered with an enormous collection of signed photographs and newspaper clippings about Antoine's and its illustrious guests. These spill over into several other rooms as well, until there doesn't seem to be an inch of space remaining for those that are bound to appear in the future.

The menu, remaining virtually unchanged for fifty years and still printed entirely in French, offers many world-renowned dishes created either on the premises or in France by the Alciatores. Those visitors who feel utterly helpless when confronted with two whole pages of French willingly put themselves in the hands of their waiters, who take this opportunity to introduce them to Antoine's magnificent gourmet fare instead of the usual steak-and-potatoes. And that's just the way Antoine's wants it to be!

The waiters, who never write down an order, play an extremely important role. Regular customers demand their own waiters when making a reservation—indeed, there are those who actually refuse to come if their waiter is unavailable. Some of these men have been with the restaurant most of their lives—the captain having worked at Antoine's for an incredible sixty-two years.

The famous Oysters Rockefeller served on a bed of hot rock salt, the fabulous Soufflé Potatoes in their special little paniers,* and the

* Made of woven strips of potatoes, French fried, and inserted in a base of bread.

blue flames of burning brandy as the Café Brûlot and Crêpes Suzettes are made at the table are all part of the magic atmosphere. The ritual attending the latter requires the dimming of the restaurant lights so that the effect can be fully appreciated—and convincing many a puzzled tourist that something is wrong with the electricity.

The list of celebrities and royalty who have dined at Antoine's fills many, many pages—in fact, few citizens would consider leaving the Crescent City without this memorable experience. Florenz Ziegfeld's favorite dish was Frog Legs Sauté Demi-Bordelaise, and though he had never tasted them before visiting New Orleans, afterward he had hundreds of frogs shipped annually to his estate in Canada.

Antoine's obligingly produced fried catfish for the famous flier Roscoe Turner (though they may have conceivably considered it an insult to their venerable coal stove). Sarah Bernhardt adored escargots, and Caruso doted on Matelotte d'Anguille—eel stew. Grand Duke Alexis, brother of the Czar, dined on Tortue Molle à la Rupiniscoff, a soft-shelled turtle stew from a secret recipe given to Jules Alciatore by a famous Muscovite chef.

Many of the marvelous dishes on the menu were invented or brought over from France in the 1830s by founder Antoine Alciatore. He began his career at the age of twelve, working in the kitchen of the Hôtel de Noailles in Marseilles. At sixteen he was given the opportunity of preparing a rare beef ordered by Talleyrand. Impressed with his meal, Talleyrand called for Antoine and asked him the name of the magnificent dish he had just created. On an impulse, recalling his father's tales of the bloody tyrant of the French Revolution, Antoine christened it Boeuf Robespierre.

At the Hôtel de Noailles, Antoine was apprenticed to the great chef Collinet, who taught him how to make Pommes Soufflées, which Collinet had invented by accident. The occasion was a banquet celebrating the initial run of the first railroad in France. King Louis Philippe was guest of honor, and Collinet planned to serve his favorite fried potatoes. When the news came that the train had arrived, Collinet put the potatoes into the hot fat, only to learn that the King, fearing to trust his life to this new contraption, would arrive later by carriage. Desperate, Collinet removed the half-browned potatoes and put them aside. When the King at last appeared, the potatoes were returned to the hot fat, where they miraculously puffed up like small balloons! The King, of course, was delighted.

Main Dining Room, Antoine's

Antoine imported the secret of Pommes Soufflées to America. Arriving in the French city of New Orleans at the mouth of the Mississippi, he worked briefly at the St. Charles Hotel. In 1840 he opened a *pension* on St. Louis Street. In the dining room downstairs he served his guests not only Pommes Soufflées, but his own creations, Boeuf Robespierre and Dinde Talleyrand. Needless to say, food-loving New Orleanians were attracted in growing numbers, and although he continued to rent rooms upstairs to performers from the French Opera House, gradually the restaurant began to take precedence over the *pension*, ultimately becoming the Antoine's that we know today.

Antoine had several sons. Jules took an early interest in the restaurant, beginning his apprenticeship in the kitchen. Alexandre worked in accounting, and Fernand opened his own restaurant, La Louisiane, in competition with Antoine's. Fernand succeeded so well that he became a serious rival, and there were many family discussions about which restaurant was better. However, when Fernand died, La Louisiane was sold, passing through a number of different managements until, under the present aegis of Moran's, its name finally vanished from the restaurant scene.

Jules Alciatore, succeeding his father in management of the restaurant, is credited with the invention of many of Antoine's most famous dishes. One that might be considered a collaboration between Jules and Antoine is Pompano en Papillote. In preparation for a banquet honoring the great Brazilian balloonist Alberto Santos-Dumont, the committee requested a special dish to commemorate the occasion—something suggesting a balloon. When Jules had difficulty with this challenge, his eighty-year-old mother told him about an invention of his father's called Pompano Montgolfier in honor of the brothers who invented the first balloon in 1783. Jules set to work at once to recreate his father's fish-in-a-paper-bag, cutting a folded, heart-shaped container which resembled the balloons of that day. Into the oiled paper went the pompano fillet, with its rich wine-flavored shrimp sauce—and out came a major culinary triumph.

Pompano en Papillote was served to Franklin D. Roosevelt at Antoine's, with champagne substituted for the white wine in its ingredients.

Cecil B. De Mille was so fond of the dish that when he was in Louisiana to film *The Buccaneer* he included it in the movie. Lyle Saxon (author of the book *Lafitte the Pirate*), who was being paid a handsome fee as technical adviser, tried to restrain De Mille on historical grounds. "Pompano en Papillote did not exist in Lafitte's time," Saxon objected. "I know, but it's so *good*" was De Mille's rejoinder. And he left it in.

Jules's most famous invention was Oysters Rockefeller, the restaurant's specialty. Every order that goes out of the kitchen bears the number of its serving, now well into the millions, and the recipe is a jealously guarded secret. (Nearly every New Orleans restaurant has its own version, most containing spinach, which is *not* an ingredient of Antoine's recipe.) Jules Alciatore conceived Oysters Rockefeller to replace the Snails Bourgignon served by Antoine's in the 1850s. Rather than import snails from France, he decided to use the plentiful and succulent New Orleans oysters, and developed an adaptation of the snail sauce appropriate to the oyster. The sauce, made up of eighteen ingredients, including absinthe, was so rich that it was named after America's wealthiest citizen.

Another creation of Jules Alciatore's came about because a lady changed her mind. In selecting a menu for the luncheon she was planning, the hostess chose fresh pineapple for dessert. During the course of the meal she decided she'd prefer to finish with an Omelette Historiée. Jules was faced with a surplus of pineapple. He simmered a thick slice in its own juice until it was golden brown, covered it with a broiled lamb chop, poured over a variation of Béarnaise sauce, and topped it with a broiled fresh mushroom. The delicious result was christened Côtelette Hawaii.

Jules is said to have borne a specially prepared tureen of soup nightly to the dressing room of Sarah Bernhardt when she played at the Old French Opera House. At the last performance she kissed him good-by and told him that if her New Orleans engagement had been a success it was because he had provided the strength for her to make it so.

Jules had two sons, Jules and Roy. Roy assumed that his elder brother would succeed his father in the now-famous restaurant. With the usual perversity of children in exhibiting indifference to their parents' established professions, neither son showed the slightest interest in the business. Jules became a professor of Romance languages. Roy was a ham-radio enthusiast, and his ambition was to be a ship's radio operator. His father offered him the opportunity to work in the kitchen at Antoine's to raise the money he needed to buy radio equipment. He began by peeling vegetables, and worked his way up to chef's helper, first in broiling, then soups, and finally making sauces. Once stimulated, the Alciatore talent took hold, and fortunately for Antoine's, New Orleans, and the world in general, Roy followed the family tradition and became a great restaurateur like his father and his grandfather. He took over Antoine's when Jules retired, and has been in charge ever since.* He has the tremendous family gift—of knowing "what foods have an affinity for each other." He experiments at home in the creation of new dishes—beginning with a basic sauce and making variations, with wines and garnishes, adding truffles, mushrooms, quenelles, or whatever he feels has a reason to be there.

Most of the dishes he has invented have been served on one occasion only, at the special dinners of the gourmet organizations, the Chevaliers du Tastevin, the Wine and Food Society, and Escargots Orleanais. At each of these affairs dedicated to food, new creations

* Ably assisted by his cousin, manager Angelo Alciatore.

Rex
REX
REX
REX 1970
REX 1971
REX 1972
REX
REX

are necessary to spark the interest of the connoisseur members. Until now these gourmet delights devised by Mr. Alciatore have been enjoyed once and then relegated to oblivion. However, now he has generously agreed to share some of them with us in this book, which is indeed cause for rejoicing.

Although the Antoine menu has remained almost unchanged for more than fifty years, Roy Alciatore has made one notable contribution; Pigeonneaux Paradis. This is a dish that he enjoyed in France during one of his periodic tours. He felt that it would be a success at Antoine's, so without asking for the recipe he returned to New Orleans and made his own version.

Another of his innovations is a physical one: the Rex Room.* The past Kings of Mardi Gras often met at Antoine's to discuss plans for the coming year. In 1942, Roy conceived the idea of converting a storeroom into a special dining room devoted to Mardi Gras. Outside the entrance to the room hang photographs of former Kings and Queens with their courts. Inside are glass cases filled with Mardi Gras memorabilia: original costume designs from the 1890s, elaborate antique invitations to Carnival balls, jewels and medals worn by Queens and members of Rex dating from 1872. Down one wall is a procession of matching gold frames filled with photographs of every past King of Mardi Gras, with empty frames bearing dates up to the year 1973, awaiting future Kings.

The Kings have absolute priority for this room, even over a previous reservation. And every year during Mardi Gras week it is a tradition for the past Mardi Gras Queens to hold a luncheon there.

Vying in popularity for private parties is the tiny, dark red 1840 Room (setting of the best-selling novel *Dinner at Antoine's*). Decorated in appropriate Victorian style, it is a reproduction of a dining room of the period in which Antoine's was founded, and is filled with family mementos. Its walls are hung with portraits of the Alciatores, menus dating back to the early '80s, old theater programs with Antoine advertisements dating from 1852, and even the founder's baby shoes!

The Mystery Room, at the end of a narrow flagstone corridor opposite the 1840 Room, displays the portraits of six Presidents who dined there. The room derived its name from the mysterious disappearance of a painting from its walls. Its door to the street was

* Also, the recently opened Proteus Room, for the Proteus carnival organization.

Rex Room, Antoine's

Kitchen, Antoine's

opened only once, to permit Franklin D. Roosevelt to enter directly from his car outside.

Adjacent to the Mystery Room is the Dungeon Room, named for its function under the Spaniards, who used some of the buildings that make up Antoine's as their military headquarters when they occupied New Orleans. The Alciatores found Spanish cannons mounted in the back yard behind the kitchen. This yard was the site of the Spanish stables, and there remains today a hidden passage under a staircase.

At the rear, in one of several small dining rooms, there is an iron grillwork gate, through which one gets an astonishing view of Antoine's wine cellar, one of the finest in the Western Hemisphere. A narrow 158 feet long, it has its temperature perfectly maintained by air conditioning against New Orleans' hot climate.

All the rooms surrounding the main dining room were added gradually as the restaurant grew. The third- and fourth-floor rooms, which once were occupied by the actors and actresses of the French Opera House, are now used only for storage. On the second floor, which was originally filled with private dining rooms, one room that has remained in use for many years has enjoyed a recent lavish redecoration worthy of its historic wood paneling. This paneling came from the old St. Louis Hotel, where it lined the walls of the room which served as the first capitol of Louisiana. Hence, this lovely private dining room on the second floor of Antoine's is called the Capitol Room.

There have been three chefs during the three generations of Alciatores, two French and one Italian. There is one artist in Antoine's kitchen whose sole responsibility is turning out Pommes Soufflées. To those adventurous souls who aspire to reproduce these fantastic potatoes—heed this warning: even Antoine's full-time potato-inflater throws away about half of those he attempts to turn out. The potatoes must be just the right kind, texture, and season (fall potatoes are best), and as Roy Alciatore wryly remarks, you even have to have the cooperation of the potato!

Roy Alciatore deserves tremendous admiration for the magnificent job he has done in the unenviable task of living up to a century-old, world-wide reputation: it is an awesome responsibility.

Main Entrance, Arnaud's

Arnaud's

A large and immensely popular French Quarter restaurant sprawling across almost the entire 800 block of Bienville Street, Arnaud's was started by the ebullient "Count" Arnaud in 1920. Arnaud was born Léon Bertrand Arnaud Cazenave in the French village of Bosdarros, on the outskirts of the city of Pau, residence of the Kings of Navarre; a village bordered by the Pyrenees and encircled by vineyards. After completing his education in Paris at the Lycée Napoleon, Cazenave decided to come to America, where he hoped to study medicine. When he arrived in the United States, he found that his English was insufficient for him to enter medical school, so he enrolled at St. Stanislaus College in Bay St. Louis, Mississippi, to study in preparation for his medical education. However, he soon realized that he would not be able to afford the years of college necessary for becoming a doctor, so he put to use his knowledge of the vineyards of France as a salesman of wines and champagnes. In his travels he discovered that New Orleans, which reminded him of his native land, was the place he wanted to settle down and live.

When an opportunity arose to lease the Old Absinthe House, he opened a café, where he began serving French food with a small bottle of wine accompanying it as "lagniappe" (an old New Orleans custom of giving something extra as a gift to the purchaser of one's goods).

Cazenave dreamed of owning his own restaurant, and although he never achieved his medical career, he fulfilled his second ambition when he opened Arnaud's Restaurant in 1920. Then it was at 811 Bienville Street, but it has since grown and spread through almost the entire block from Bourbon to Dauphine Street. The first chef was a woman, Madame Pierre, who was said to have been a sorceress with French and Spanish food. At her death, Madame Pierre was succeeded by Louis Lamothe and Jean Laune, both pupils of the chef of Napoleon III. They were followed in turn by Jean Baptiste Lauhle, who by coincidence was born in Arnaud's native village in France.

Although chefs have an obvious importance in the cuisine of any restaurant, it was Arnaud himself who molded the personality of his establishment and influenced the food that it produced. A *bon vivant*, an epicure, with a distinctive style, Arnaud would often imagine dishes that he fancied would enhance his menu. He would make notes of these ideas and send them to the chef prefaced with the remarks "I am not a cook—I give you the outline. We will improve or change if necessary." After this he and the chef experimented until they achieved the desired results. In this manner the non-cooking Arnaud (said to be a steak-and-potatoes man himself) invented the following dishes: Shrimp Arnaud (with the renowned and much imitated sauce—so popular that it is sold in bottles), Filet de Truite Vendôme, Oysters Bienville, Supreme de Volaille en Papillote, Heart of Artichoke en Surprise, Filet Mignon Clemenceau, Chicken Victoria, Monts d'Amour Rosalinde, and Crêpes Suzettes Arnaud. He also conceived many notable and popular drinks, among them the French 75 and Ambrosia—the drink of the gods—which he loved to send to favorite friends at their tables as they finished dinner. Arnaud was justly proud of his cellar, which has the distinction of being the only one in New Orleans that is actually underground.

Arnaud earned the affectionate title of Count because of his courtly style, his elegant wardrobe, the carnation in his buttonhole, the way he flourished his cigar. His infectious enthusiasm for serving fine food and his exuberant friendliness won him many friends.

He believed that cooking was an art and "the soul of festivity at all times and to all ages," and he liked to quote Corneille: "*Il y a tant de maîtresses. . . . Il n'y a qu'un diner.*"

The Count used to start the day with a pint of champagne for breakfast, and finish it with endless cups of coffee laced with 50 per cent bourbon. In his later years his doctor ordered him to give up his morning champagne for a pint of orange juice. The irrepressible Count compromised by drinking his pint of orange juice mixed with a pint of champagne.

The Count lived in a style befitting his "title" in a grand twenty-three room house on Esplanade Avenue, with a grilled iron gate, a gold drawing room, twelve bathrooms, a swimming pool on the roof, and a tower from which he could watch Mardi Gras parades. Amid this grandeur he had for himself a monastic room where he kept glass cases filled with medical books.

It was in this gilded cage that he tried to contain his bird of paradise daughter, Germaine. It was his ambition to "make a lady" of his only daughter, and, in fact, Arnaud and Germaine reigned (separately) as King and Queen of many Carnival balls. But peppery, dark, and dynamic Germaine demonstrated an early flair for the theatrical. She won a state-wide talent contest and as the prize, went off on a cross-country tour of the RKO vaudeville circuit. After a period of studying voice in Paris, she returned to New Orleans to sing with the San Carlo Opera Company and act at Le Petit Théâtre du Vieux Carré. She likes to compare the restaurant business to the theater, where every evening the curtain goes up and "you're on."

Germaine was never trained by her father to manage the restaurant, and many (including the Count himself) thought that the establishment might die with Arnaud. However, after Arnaud Cazenave's passing in 1948, and a brief period of proprietorship by her mother, Germaine fooled them all by taking over the reins of the formidable institution that Arnaud's Restaurant had become, and continuing its past success.

Arnaud's employs a staff of 150 people and can seat fifteen hundred diners. There are eight cooks in the kitchen working on shrimp alone, and twenty other chefs besides. The extraordinary variety of the menu has been further expanded by Germaine, who seems to have inherited her father's flair for creating new gustatory treats. She invented Twelfth Night Flambée (in honor of the Twelfth Night commencement of the Carnival season)—Rock Cornish hen stuffed with wild rice and imported pâté de foie gras, which arrives at the table flaming dramatically. Other innovations credited to the Count's flamboyant daughter are Canapé à la Irma (named after her mother), Pineapple Flambée, Apple Pie Flambée à la Magdelene, and Water Cress Salad à la Germaine. Among the fantastic new drinks that she has concocted are the Beauty and the Beast and the Germaine Cocktail, the latter described by its namesake as Triple Sec, gin, bourbon, champagne, orange juice, and ice mixed together and "shaken like hell."

Germaine has carried her devotion to her parents and her flair for the dramatic into the restaurant itself. In the rear of the building she has established the Carnival Room (it is actually *two* rooms) through which visitors to the restaurant will be ushered with due solemnity and ceremony, if they so desire. Lining the walls across from the entrance are elaborate examples of her mother's crochet work. Inside, displayed in glass cases, are mannequins in full regalia,

Carnival Room, Arnaud's

dressed in the costumes (one-of-a-kind for one occasion only) that Arnaud wore as King and Germaine wore as Queen of numerous Carnival balls. There are also costumes, graduating in size from a six-year-old's, that Germaine's daughter wore as page, attendant, and finally Queen (with a genuine ermine-trimmed train). Flanking the costumes are photographs showing scenes of the balls at which the costumes were worn, and flanking these are glass cases filled with accessories, such as goblets and scepters. Germaine's most memorable appearance as Queen was dedicated to a food motif, with her maids arrayed as Shrimp Arnaud and other dishes made famous at her father's restaurant.

Germaine has also instituted an annual Easter parade that culminates in an Easter dinner at Arnaud's. Inspired by an Easter visit to St. Patrick's Cathedral in New York, this New Orleans counterpart begins at the St. Louis Cathedral at Jackson Square. After the

Easter service, Germaine and her guests embark in flower-festooned, horse-drawn carriages and parade through the streets of the French Quarter in all their Easter finery to the doors of Arnaud's. There, accompanied by musicians playing in the street, Germaine is greeted and handed down by the mayor, who joins her and her guests inside for the Easter dinner.

Evidently believing that variety is the spice of life, Germaine has devised a scheme of making each Easter dinner, with its special menu (designed by herself) an international occasion—such as a Basque Easter, a Hawaiian Easter, or a Hong Kong Easter. The food, of course is in keeping with the theme, with sukiyaki, tempura, or whatever may be appropriate. The festivities are further enlivened by prizes, given periodically during the afternoon for the best Easter hats worn by lady guests.

Arnaud's has received many honors. One of the most notable was the invitation to participate in a week-long celebration of the two

Easter Parade, Arnaud's

thousandth anniversary of the founding of Paris. Held at the Chambord Restaurant in New York, the "noble tradition of French cuisine" was saluted with a "Gourmet Festival." This included five weeks of cooking presided over by a different guest chef each week, presenting the specialties of his own restaurant. Arnaud's chef, Jean Pierre, presided over the third week, in such exalted company as chefs from Maxim's of Paris and the Pump Room of Chicago.

Germaine has traveled about the country to various conventions and festivities of the food and drink business, receiving awards and compliments, such as an accolade from the *maître d'hotel* at the Plaza's Oak Room, who called her a true connoisseur of food. The walls of Arnaud's main dining room are lined with autographed photographs of movie stars paying tribute to the meals they enjoyed there. Among the blown-up newspaper clippings that are interspersed among the photographs there is a wartime news story about a Louisiana company on an island in the South Pacific. The lieutenant in charge found a new and remarkable cook who could do fantastic things with Army rations, and in appreciation of his skill, the lieutenant christened the officers' mess as a namesake of his favorite restaurant back home "La Petite Maison Arnaud"!

Brennan's

Brennan's is unquestionably the most glamorous and handsome of the New Orleans restaurants. It has the romance and candlelight, the patio and curving stairways, and all the trappings that have always been the dream image of New Orleans' French Quarter—when actually such a setting never existed there before Owen Brennan created it.

Brennan's Restaurant might be called a prodigy on the New Orleans scene, having been born only in 1946; its history is like a Horatio Alger story.

Second-generation American, born of a family which was driven to America's shores by Ireland's potato famine, Owen Brennan grew up on the other side of the tracks in New Orleans' Irish Channel. He drifted from job to job—candy-factory worker, manager of a filling station and a drugstore, liquor salesman. In the last capacity, he became friendly with the owner of the Court of Two Sisters, a restaurant and nightclub built around a charming old courtyard. When the proprietor was forced to go off to war, he asked Owen to manage the business in his absence. Aided by the booming wartime economy and his gregarious personality, Owen made a smashing success of it. He was ready and eager to go into business for himself when he heard that the franchise on the Old Absinthe House was for sale. Owen bought it immediately and continued, and even multiplied, his previous successes at the Court of Two Sisters. The Absinthe House was an ancient, crumbling building (since restored) on Bourbon Street, surrounded by legends associated with Lafitte the pirate, and it has had a varied career since originally housing a leather-goods store. In the 1860s it became a restaurant featuring absinthe, which was dripped* on a long marble bar. It had its ups and

* In a device such as the one illustrated opposite, water was dripped from the ice-filled glass globe into the absinthe, thereby (through some mysterious chemical reaction) increasing its potency.

Façade, Brennan's

downs under changing managements and rising and falling degrees of popularity, including a period as a nightclub, and also as a restaurant run by Arnaud Cazenave, founder of Arnaud's Restaurant. It was a custom at the Old Absinthe House for guests to tack their calling cards on the walls of the bar, and eventually the entire interior was papered with layers of them, in various shades of brown and yellow depending on their age.

Owen made much of the Secret Room, a kind of half story built between the second and third floors, that had given rise to the myth that Lafitte and Andrew Jackson met there. Brennan exhibited his developing genius for publicity by setting up cannons and historically garbed mannequins to take advantage of these legends.

He began a policy of bringing name entertainers to the city—beginning with Ethel Waters. However, it was "Fats" Pichon, a talented and enormously popular Negro pianist, playing under a tilted mirror suspended from the ceiling, who really made the Absinthe House the place to go in the French Quarter. It caught on not only with New Orleanians, but with visiting celebrities as well. Earl Wilson and Robert Ruark became regular customers, along with many movie stars who came to try Owen's wild concoction, the Pirate's Dream—a fantastic drink made of several kinds of rum and fruit juices, served in a huge glass with many straws.

It was at the Absinthe House that Owen began to bring other members of the family into the business. It started with his handsome, redheaded sister Adelaide, who was put in charge of bookkeeping in an office upstairs. Brennan didn't really approve of having his sister work in a bar, so he not only limited her schedule to the daytime but brought his younger sister, Ella, along as a kind of chaperone.

The Absinthe House did so well that Owen Brennan (dared, so the story goes, by Count Arnaud, who teased him about the Irish lack of knowledge of fine cooking) decided to open a restaurant. He took over the Vieux Carré Restaurant, also on Bourbon Street and housed in one of the oldest buildings in the city. Owen immediately changed the name to Brennan's Vieux Carré, and it was not long

Brennan's Carriageway

before the fame of this infant version of the present Brennan's Restaurant began to grow and spread throughout the city and the country. Now the whole Brennan clan began to take part, as Owen's father joined him in partnership, and Adelaide, Ella, and brother John expanded their responsibilities from the Absinthe House. Adelaide continued in charge of accounting, and John managed the buying. Ella started working as a substitute cashier, but she became so capable at overseeing the waiters, and had so many definite ideas about the cuisine, that Owen finally turned over the direction of the kitchen to his teen-age sister. Ella objected to serving only the same dishes that all the other restaurants featured. She wanted to develop a character for Brennan's food that was theirs alone. She tried to work with the chef in introducing new recipes, but he was inflexible, so she fired him and promoted his assistant, Paul Blangé, who remained head chef through all of Brennan's formative years. Together Ella and Paul Blangé evolved a new and distinctive cuisine by digging through ancient cookbooks and working out their versions of the recipes they chose. Their Trout Blangé, Chicken Pontalba, and Crêpes Fitzgerald are only a few examples of the dishes they created that really belong to Brennan's.

Breakfast at Brennan's, now an institution, was conceived by Owen with the help of Lucius Beebe. Perhaps it was an unconscious throwback to the days of those Sunday morning orgies at Begué's. In any event, it attained immediate popularity. A lordly meal resembling a brunch, it starts with a drink such as Absinthe Suissesse, continues with a fruit, like grilled grapefruit, followed by one of Brennan's marvelous egg dishes—Royale, Sardou, Hussarde, etc., hot French bread, a dessert such as Bananas Foster, and, of course, New Orleans coffee. Breakfast at Brennan's became such a trademark that the colorful cock on a red background was designed to decorate their menus, match folders, and billboards.

Owen Brennan's genius for inventions such as Breakfast at Brennan's was only one part of the secret of his success. His effervescent charm, his friendliness and geniality, and his unfailing welcome to any visiting celebrity played a large part in the smash hit that Brennan's scored. He even had a special guest room over the Old Absinthe House where he could offer hospitality to friends like Robert Ruark, who expressed his appreciation in many enthusiastic syndicated newspaper columns. When an out-of-town VIP was in residence, Owen would shower his guest with attentions, such as special meals and drinks sent up on the impulse of sincere friendliness and generosity. This kind of public relations could not fail to bear fruit, especially when coupled with fine food, graciously served in a handsome setting (Brennan always favored candlelight and deep carpets, even in the Vieux Carré Restaurant).

The result was that the Brennans decided to expand into larger quarters to accommodate their booming business. They took over the building called Patio Royal at 417 Royal Street, and proceeded to have it done over by the most esteemed New Orleans architects, Richard Koch and Sam Wilson.

The building had a fascinating history, curiously linked with misfortune. In fact, Owen Brennan was considered brave, or even foolhardy, to move into it, as it seemed to have a permanent jinx on it. Built as a residence in 1801, it is said to have been designed by the leading architect of the day, Benjamin Latrobe. First his son and then Latrobe himself died in the New Orleans yellow-fever epidemic. The first owner of the house, Faurie, sold it to the Bank of Louisiana, whose initials still decorate the iron grillwork. The next owner was Martin Gordon, whom Andrew Jackson visited there in 1828. Gordon lost his fortune, but a subsequent Jackson appointment took him to Washington, and the house became the property of Judge Morphy. Morphy's son Paul became at a very early age the world's greatest chess player, but he died as a young man, in a state of complete mental and physical breakdown. Following Morphy, the building was owned by a wealthy art patron named Irby, who met his end by suicide—supposedly shooting himself over the coffin he had selected. He left the building to Tulane University, and the University leased it to a series of unsuccessful restaurants, the last of which was the Patio Royal.

Apparently the jinx worked its evil on the Brennans, too, because during the early stages of the renovation of the building Owen Brennan died suddenly in his sleep of a heart attack.

The members of the Brennan family pulled themselves together after this terrible loss and made up their minds to carry on. They determined to open on the day that Owen had scheduled—between breakfast and lunch, just as he had planned.

It must have been quite a sight, the musical-comedy climax to this rags-to-riches success story, when Brennan's best customers (including some of the city's elite in business and society) unexpectedly turned up to help carry the chairs and silverware through the streets in the rain to the new restaurant, led by a jazz band playing "When the Saints Go Marching In." Maybe they helped to exorcise the evil spirits, because after this auspicious beginning there has been nothing but good fortune in the jinxed "old Morphy house."

Ella and Adelaide have continued to run the business, assisted by brother Dick and Owen, Jr. As anyone who has eaten there will attest, the food is fabulous, with special emphasis on dramatic flaming desserts cooked at the table, and constant innovations in the menu. Not content with merely enjoying their fame and popularity, the Brennans are always thinking of new ways to please the customers. For instance, a new "Cool" menu was devised for the summer months. Not only is the menu printed in green instead of the familiar Brennan red, but the waiters' jackets are changed from red to green, and so is the striped awning over the carriageway.

The already gorgeous decor is always being added to, with a gold sconce here, an antique picture there. There is a red plush-lined

Brennan's Courtyard

A Dining Room, Brennan's

phone booth—and a lavender *bidet* in the ladies room! Almost all the lovely dining rooms overlook the lush green patio (where only drinks are served) and in any part of the restaurant it is impossible to imagine a more elegant way to dine.

In 1963 Brennan's invited all the winners of the coveted annual *Holiday* Magazine Award for Dining Distinction to a gala dinner. Over a hundred came from all points of the compass, accompanied by husbands and wives. They were met with champagne at the airport by members of the Brennan clan, and honored with the feast that follows the end of this chapter. This affair was such a success (and no mean feat for an audience of the country's finest restaurateurs) that it set a precedent. Now there is a dinner in a different city each year for the *Holiday* Award winners, though no longer does any one restaurant bear the entire cost and responsibility as Brennan's did.

Also in 1963, the Brennans expanded their operations with the acquisition of another restaurant called Friendship House, on the Gulf Coast, and the latest addition to the Brennan empire is a replica of the New Orleans Brennan's in Houston, Texas.

Brennan's has already had its own cookbook for several years, but since there have been new and delectable dishes added to the menu, some additional recipes which have not appeared before are included in this book. Though dining at home is no substitute for the pleasure of eating at Brennan's, many thousands of people who have used its cookbook have discovered that the recipes make the transition from restaurant to home with superlative results.

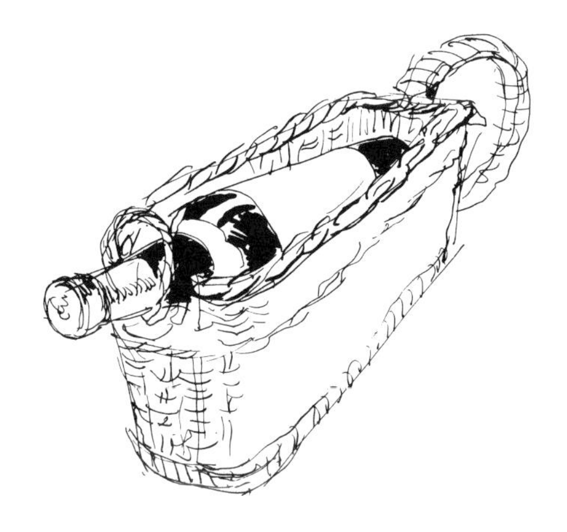

Menu of Brennan's Dinner
HONORING RECIPIENTS OF THE *HOLIDAY* MAGAZINE AWARD

Les Huîtres à la Holiday
Tattinger 1959
Livermore Pinot Blanc, Wente

*

Le Bisque d'Écrevisses
Victoria Dry Bobadilla Sherry

*

Les Crabes Buster Béarnaise
Meursault Perrières 1962

*

Les Pigeonneaux Acadiens
Château Margaux 1953
Le Riz à la Louisiane
Okra Evangeline

*

Salade de Saison

*

Les Bons Fromages Américains
Monterey Jack de Californie
Meunster du Wisconsin
Brie de l'Illinois

*

Les Bananes à la Foster
Bollinger 1955
Café à la Nouvelle Orleans

Galatoire's

Galatoire's holds perhaps the highest accolade of all—it is the overwhelming favorite of the citizens of New Orleans. Completely unpretentious in its decor, modest, and publicity shy (no advertising ever), it exists only to prepare and serve fine food. Galatoire's has maintained for years an unswerving policy of "no reservations," and no amount of fame, prestige, or influence will persuade the proprietors to alter it. The physical appearance of the restaurant and almost everything about its management have remained the same since its inception at the turn of the century. The surroundings on Bourbon Street have undergone a considerable metamorphosis since Jean Galatoire bought the business from Victor Bero in 1905, but once you step inside the swinging green-curtained front door and see the white-tiled floor, the old-fashioned coat racks and hooks, the ceiling fans, the old clock and desk, you could easily imagine (except for the air conditioning that now cools the tropical atmosphere) that you were back in the era when Bourbon Street was a fashionable residential area instead of the notoriously gaudy midway that it is today.

When the city of New Orleans was planned and laid out by Bienville, Bourbon Street was named in honor of the royal family of France. It became a street of stately homes of colonial residents. The Cosmopolitan Hotel, which was in the first block off Canal Street, housed the Chess, Checkers and Whist Club. Judah P. Benjamin, Secretary of State of the Confederacy (and often called the "brains of the Confederacy") lived in the house at 327 Bourbon Street. At 516, the noted writer Lafcadio Hearn lived in 1878, in the beautiful old home of Jean Baptiste Lefebre. The famous Quadroon Balls were said to have taken place on Bourbon Street in the old Orleans Theatre, which had a very large ballroom. Most notable and influential of all, however, was the French Opera House, the cultural and social center of the city. There all theatrical and operatic events took place; Sarah Bernhardt performed, and Adelina

Façade, Galatoire's

Patti is said to have made her debut there. After her opening her admirers pulled her carriage through the streets to express their adulation in true Mediterranean style. The early Carnival balls were held in the French Opera House, and the daughters of the Creole aristocracy made their debuts within its fashionable walls.

The building burned in 1919, a loss for which the city has never really compensated, and Bourbon Street began to deteriorate. The street commenced its gradual decline as some of the fine old houses became partially commercial, with stores, coffeehouses, and restaurants on the ground floors. At the beginning of the twentieth century many of the mansions were turned into houses of ill repute or "cribs." Jazz was born as entertainment in the "fancy houses." Most of these finally left Bourbon for Basin Street, in the heyday of Storyville, and the street reverted to restaurants, antique shops, and studio apartments. For a brief period Bourbon Street resumed its past respectability, but in the Roaring 20s it became what it is today, the home of jazz, strip-tease joints, honky-tonks—complete with barkers, neon, and lewd photographs.

Galatoire's almost seems to have been left on Bourbon Street by accident, a relic of what used to be in the gaslight days when Creole aristocrats in evening clothes arrived in their carriages at the French Opera House. All the turmoil and change swirling about its doors, however, has affected it not one bit.

Jean Galatoire came to America from France as a young man. He went at first to Birmingham to live, but finding no French colony in Alabama, he rather naturally gravitated to New Orleans, where he started a restaurant in the French Quarter on Dauphine Street. In 1905 (at least this is the date the Galatoires remember, although there is a New Orleans guidebook printed in 1893 that lists Galatoire's Restaurant at 209 Bourbon!) Jean Galatoire bought Victor's Restaurant, which had been established by Victor Bero in 1830. It has been run by the Galatoire family ever since.

When Jean Galatoire bought the restaurant there were hams and game hanging in the front windows. He made it into a typical small French restaurant; in fact, it resembles many of the average Parisian restaurants of today. Jean hired French chefs, and many of his fine dishes have been passed on from one chef to another without ever having been written down. Originally there were private dining rooms upstairs, and many of the big men in the cotton business began eating there. They spread the word about Galatoire's good food, and the gourmet New Orleanians adopted it enthusiastically. It became a custom for Canal Street's merchant princes to eat together at a long table in front of the clock at the rear of the dining room. As Galatoire's has never allowed its quality to change, neither has the enthusiasm of the people of New Orleans waned.

Jean Galatoire's nephews—Justin, Léon, and Gabriel—were his heirs and successors in the restaurant. Justin began in the business when he was nineteen, and is still there today. He and his brothers took over in 1916, when Jean Galatoire retired.

Chris Ansell was Justin's son-in-law, married to one of his four daughters—and an enthusiastic worker at Galatoire's. He took particular pride in the *Holiday* Magazine Awards that had been presented to the restaurant each year. In fact, he was in a television studio, ready for the award-presentation ceremony, at which he was representing the Galatoire family, when he died of a heart attack. The family and the many friends of the restaurant were understandably shaken, and have scarcely recovered from the blow. However, with Mr. Justin, his daughter Yvonne and her husband, and Léon's two sons, there seems to be no lack of Galatoires to carry on the family business.

This kind of clannish solidarity and devotion—not to mention character—has resulted in a dependable and unfailing quality that is virtually without equal. The character that molds the personality of the restaurant is unquestionably Mr. Justin's. Mr. Justin is a marvelously friendly man who loves people. He has a knack for being sympathetic and congenial, so that he is able to communicate equally well with all kinds of people, each on his own level. He is thoroughly dedicated to the best in food and wines without pretension—he disapproves of conserving certain years and vintages in a cellar to impress customers. He is devoted to fairness to all and refuses to make exceptions to his standing rule of no reservations.

One night during a busy season when there was a line of people waiting outside all the way to the corner, a man burst into Galatoire's and went back to the desk looking for the owner. He found Mr. Justin and explained indignantly that he was the governor of a state and not accustomed to waiting in line for a table for dinner. "Do you believe in fairness?" Mr. Justin asked him. Of course the governor had to answer in the affirmative. So Mr. Justin explained that it would not be fair for him to give a table to the governor while all the other citizens waited in line.

Actor Charles Laughton was also upset one night when he was confronted with a line of some seventy-odd people before him at the doors to Galatoire's. In his inimitable Captain Bligh manner, Mr. Laughton made known his displeasure at this state of affairs. Undaunted and unintimidated, Mr. Justin stood his ground and explained to Laughton that if he didn't want to wait, the best time to come for dinner was five o'clock in the afternoon. Laughton came next day at five, and several times thereafter.

By the same token, Galatoire's has always been closed for business on Mondays. The management refuses to vary this routine even on the busiest Monday of the year, the day before Mardi Gras.

Although they had ample opportunity to change their modest and simple decor following a disastrous $75,000 fire in 1956 (and an earlier one as well), the Galatoires worked night and day for two weeks to reopen, with everything restored exactly as it was before.

Perhaps the greatest "secret" of the Galatoires' success (and undoubtedly a rare, if not unique custom in the restaurant world) is their insistence on entirely fresh food every single day. Each morning the Galatoires order from their local suppliers just the amount of food that they think will carry them through to the end of that day. Perhaps they might run out of crabmeat or trout, for instance, but they are careful not to have any left over for tomorrow. Although some restaurants get their meat from Chicago, or have lobster flown in from Maine, Galatoire's buys only fresh local products on a daily basis. Not content with this guarantee of freshness, the chefs and the Galatoires themselves carefully inspect the crabmeat, the fish, and the meats as they come in in the morning to make sure they are of the finest and freshest quality. If they fail to pass the test, they go back. Mr. Justin himself used to be there early in the morning peeling the shrimp and picking crabmeat. The wine selection is careful, too. Mr. Justin believes in having just a small stock of wines and liquors, but only the very best. The waiters themselves mix the drinks, with no bartender and no checking-out system. The waiters, as a matter of fact, are an important factor in the enduring success of the restaurant. The Galatoires believe that if you want your employees to enjoy their work you have to be good to them—thus they have a great deal of loyalty from their staff. They have a ratio of seventeen waiters to forty tables, which ensures that each waiter is able to devote ample attention to his customers. And they *are* his customers; for at Galatoire's (and Antoine's as well) the waiter has an importance that is unparalleled elsewhere. The waiters are not assigned to stations as in most restaurants. Instead, regular customers acquire their favorite waiters, forming lasting relationships. A customer will therefore not only ask for, but insist on being served by *his* waiter. It is not unusual to hear the customers and waiters gossiping about family affairs like old friends while the meal is being served. Many of these will be able to anticipate what their customers want without asking. Also, if a customer wants to try a dish a different way, the waiter will make it for him; for instance, one of the waiters improvised a dessert for his customer—vanilla ice cream topped with chocolate sauce and crème de menthe. Sometimes these newly invented dishes become part of the menu, but sometimes only one's own waiter will know about them. There is a Godchaux Salad and a Gus Mayer Salad, made up by waiters at the request of two of the city's leading merchants. The Crêpe Maison (a crêpe rolled with jelly and almonds, covered with orange liqueur) was devised by one of the waiters and is now listed on the menu.

There's no doubt at all that the pace has quickened in slow and easygoing New Orleans. Bourbon Street has certainly changed, and the Galatoires no longer have neighbors sitting on rockers on the sidewalk outside their door. But people have been known to return to Galatoire's after an absence of twenty years, order the same food (very likely from the same waiter), and swear it is still the same. And that's the way they like it.

Corinne Dunbar's

Dunbar's is a restaurant that people love to discover. Eating there is like being invited to dinner in an elegant old Southern home. A tiny place, in an old white house on lower St. Charles Avenue, it is identified only by a small brass plaque that says "Corinne Dunbar." Its advertising is by word of mouth only, so paradoxically, there are many New Orleanians who have never been there, and yet its fame is widespread across America and even abroad. There is a story about a prominent New Orleans man who was on a trip to California. The mayor of Pasadena asked him, "How's my favorite New Orleans restaurant?" When this turned out to be Corinne Dunbar's, the New Orleanian had to admit he had never eaten there. Returning home, he phoned from the airport for a reservation!

The restaurant was started when Corinne Dunbar, a Creole aristocrat, opened her home for entertaining. The house itself, reputed to have been the home of a Civil War general, is in the once very fashionable residential area on fringes of the Garden District. The furnishings were Mrs. Dunbar's own family pieces, and the food was served on lovely china with beautiful old silver.

Mrs. Dunbar, like many another Southern lady, had a flair for cooking and entertaining. This does not necessarily mean that she ever did any cooking herself, but that she could hire, supervise, and train cooks to produce matchless dishes from her collection of old family recipes.

New Orleans society adopted Mrs. Dunbar's immediately—as a perfect place to have bridal and debutante parties, and for ladies who were shopping on the Avenue to have lunch.

After Mrs. Dunbar died, her daughter Katherine ran the restaurant for several years. However, she decided to give it up in order to devote her time to her family, so she turned the business over to Jimmie Plauché, a distant cousin, who she knew would maintain Dunbar's in its original style. Mr. Plauché added wine, cocktails, and air conditioning, but he was careful not to modernize the Victorian decor or enlarge the dining area.

Exterior, Corrine Dunbar's

Dining at Dunbar's is, of necessity, by reservation only. The guests (who must ring the doorbell) are greeted by a butler and escorted to the parlor, past a twelve-foot gilt pier mirror and framed antique Carnival invitations, where they may have their drinks. Afterward they go into the dining room—a handsome high-ceilinged room done in blue, white, and gold, with a crystal chandelier hung from an ornate gold medallion. There is no menu. The meal, served by colored girls in white uniforms, always begins with a fruit dish, served with a homemade sauce passed in a silver pitcher. The next dish at dinner (lunch is somewhat lighter) is soup. No Creole meal is complete without a hearty soup, such as Okra Gumbo, Crawfish Bisque, or Gumbo z'Herbes (a contraction of *aux herbes*). A special V-toast (designed by Mrs. Dunbar in honor of Winston Churchill) is served with the soup. Dunbar's specialty, Oysters and Artichokes, comes next—the only course that is served every day. It is accompanied by warm French bread, for dipping in the marvelous sauce.

The main course could be any one of two dozen Creole dishes—Bouillabaisse, Chicken Maitland, Grillades, Daube Creole, to name a few. Fish is served only on Friday. A procession of vegetables arrives with the meat. Guests serve themselves, and may even ask for more. Mrs. Dunbar had a special knack for making fabulous dishes out of the common carrot or ordinary spinach. Native Louisiana vegetables are especially featured, such as Plantains Caramel, Baked Cushaw, and Stuffed Mirlitons. Hot biscuits or tiny muffins are passed during the main course.

By this time no one could possibly want a large rich dessert. A small touch of sweet (the Creole word for it is *goûté*) like *petits fours* or ice cream with homemade sauce, followed by a demitasse, is the end of a typical dinner at Dunbar's.

Mr. Plauché plans all the menus with meticulous care in chart form (he has every menu for every day since he took over the restaurant) so that dishes are not repeated on the same day of the week for a long period of time.

Although the restaurant's policy is based on a set menu for each meal, it is not entirely inflexible. Dunbar's recognizes special diets and always has food on hand for such emergencies. There was a noted woman theosophist in New Orleans who entertained there regularly for two or three people. One day she had a party for eighteen, including the leading theosophist of the world. All the guests were vegetarians. Their dinner consisted of a fruit course, plain artichoke, omelet, and four vegetables—and they loved it.

During the busy winter season Dunbar's often has to turn away twice as many people as it is able to seat. One evening Albert, the butler, came to Mr. Plauché and said, "There's a man outside who wants a table for dinner." Jimmie Plauché said, "Albert, you know we haven't any more tables." Albert just stood there. Finally Mr. Plauché said, "What's the matter? Who is it?" Albert explained that it was Andre Kostelanetz, who had crept out of a banquet to dine at Dunbar's. They managed to squeeze him in.

The late Linda Darnell did the same thing. She was in town with her new husband, combining a honeymoon with a tour for charity. They left a dinner given for her to come to Dunbar's to dine alone. They planned to go back in an hour, but arrived at seven and stayed until midnight!

Oliver, a celebrity in France as the owner and chef of the world-famed restaurant Le Grand Véfour and star of a popular French television program, was the honored guest at an official dinner given

Dunbar's Dining Room

by the French Consul at Dunbar's. He had toured the United States and been feted in the best restuarants of New York and San Francisco. He complained to the French Consul before dinner in New Orleans, "But every time they take me to French restaurants. I would like to eat some American food!" He finally got his wish, and was delighted with the dinner he had at Dunbar's. He was particularly fond of jambalaya.

Another noted guest was actress Lillian Gish, in New Orleans to direct *Die Fledermaus*. When urged to try New Orleans' many famous restaurants, she told the stage manager that she didn't like restaurants. There was only one she liked—in Spain. The stage manager managed to lure Miss Gish to Dunbar's, and it made such a hit with her that she wrote afterward, "Now there are *two* fine restaurants in the world."

Guests often ask Jimmie Plauché the story of the portrait hanging in the parlor. The lady in the picture is his great-great-great-great-grandmother—and she has a remarkable history. Her parents were French plantation owners living in Santo Domingo. In her youth there was a bloody slave uprising of which she was the sole white survivor, spirited away by her nurse in a fishing boat to the coast of Florida. She then settled in Natchez—and there followed an Indian massacre. Once more she was one of a handful of survivors. She came to live in New Orleans and after that practically commuted to and from France. Some of her children were born in New Orleans and remained there, and some were born in France and became French residents. Thus two separate branches of the family were started. When Mr. Plauché's aunt wanted to marry a French count, it was discovered by accident that they were fourth cousins. Because of the peregrinations of the lady in the portrait they had to get special permission to marry.

One of the vicissitudes of any restaurant business is breakage of china and glassware, and this becomes even more of a problem in a restaurant that uses such delicate china as Dunbar's. However, the only sizable amount of breakage at Dunbar's seems to be the fragile demitasse cups. As they kept breaking, Mr. Plauché stored the saucers away, having no idea what he would do with them. Finally, when he discovered that he had some sixteen hundred and fifty demitasse saucers, he conceived the notion of having a little gold sticker made, with the inscription "Corinne Dunbar's," for the bottom of each saucer, and putting them around as ashtrays. Eight hundred

Victorian Parlor, Dunbar's

of them have disappeared in six months—as souvenirs. Presumably the breakage of cups will keep up with the need for a supply of saucers.

The only two recipes from Dunbar's that cannot appear in this book are the two specialties: Huîtres Dunbar and Beignets de Bananes. Mr. Plauché absolutely and adamantly refuses to divulge the secret—and this is completely in character with Creole custom. There is a story of an old Creole lady who confided her favorite recipe to her loyal family servant. With great ceremony and solemnity she first extracted an oath of utter, undying secrecy—that she swear never to reveal the recipe to a living soul. The old lady's memory failed, and she had to ask her servant for the recipe. "No, ma'am," was her answer, "you made me promise not to tell a living soul."

Jimmie Plauché encountered this very problem when he took over Dunbar's. Mrs. Dunbar's daughter Katherine handed him the book of family recipes, but he discovered that there was one missing: the recipe for the crystallized grapefruit rind that was so popular with after-dinner coffee. "Oh, Papa made that," Katherine told him, "and he never would tell anyone how to make it." After the guests began complaining about the lack of this delicacy, it occurred to Mr. Plauché that one of the staff used to assist Papa in its preparation. When he first approached her, she didn't think she could remember it, but at last when offered a raise in salary to produce a weekly supply she managed to come through with it successfully.

Mr. Plauché is besieged constantly by earnest and anxious pleas for his two most popular recipes, but he is not to be persuaded. One night a lawyer buttonholed him after dinner and talked to him for twenty minutes. It was a marvelously skillful peroration, like a summation in the courtroom. At the end Mr. Plauché was almost ready to give him anything he asked for, but it turned out to be the oyster recipe that he was after.

Customers have been found back in the alleyway after dinner trying to bribe the cooks for the secret. They have never succeeded because Dunbar's treats the staff so well that their loyalty is unshakable. So all of us will have to make do with the other recipes that Mr. Plauché has agreed to share with us.

Caribbean Room of the Pontchartrain Hotel

Although the Caribbean Room was originally conceived to enhance the Pontchartrain Hotel, according to owner Lysle Aschaffenburg "the tail is now wagging the dog." The Pontchartrain, which began as an apartment hotel, had no restaurant (other than a small coffee shop) until 1947, when Mr. Aschaffenburg decided that a fine hotel *must* have a fine dining room. Since that time, after going through a series of transitions it has become such a huge success that the dining area has recently emerged from a transformation and sumptuous remodeling that will double its facilities.

To understand how it got that way it is necessary to know the story and the personality of Lysle Aschaffenburg, who built it, owns it, is and always has been the shaper of the character of the Pontchartrain and its exciting restaurant.

Lysle Aschaffenburg went to Cornell University and studied mechanical engineering. Since Cornell has a famous hotel school, everyone who knows Mr. Aschaffenburg today immediately jumps to the conclusion that he went to Cornell to prepare for that profession, but when he enrolled at Cornell "the hotel school wasn't even a gleam in Mr. Statler's eye."

Although he graduated a mechanical engineer, after serving in World War I he followed his father into the real-estate business. His father had built the first high-rise apartment building in New Orleans in 1905, a second in 1907, and operated the Lafayette Hotel as well. His father died in 1918, and when Lysle Aschaffenburg returned from the war, he took over the management of these properties.

He built the Pontchartrain in 1927—which he declares ruefully was twenty-five years too soon. It opened just prior to the depression and, like 85 per cent of the hotels in America, went down with the crash. He came very close to losing the hotel entirely, as it was taken over first by the second-mortgage holder, a hotel-furniture manufacturer, and then the Manufacturers Trust Company of New York.

He managed to regain a foothold in his own hotel by buying into the second mortgage of the Manufacturers Trust. He became the nominal owner of the Pontchartrain, managing the hotel for a bondholders' committee. This arrangement lasted for a number of years, during which he tried to gain control—without the money to do it. During the 30s he heard that a syndicate was planning to buy the hotel out from under him, so he sought the help of a friend, W. Horace Williams, who financed the purchase of the Pontchartrain, and Aschaffenburg and Williams owned the building in partnership.

The Pontchartrain was at that time a residential hotel, and the only one in New Orleans. One day in the coffee shop Mr. Aschaffenburg had what he considers the most important and profitable conversation he ever had in his life, with one of the many elderly ladies who lived in his hotel. She complained that her friends told her that her rent was too high. This lady was paying $180 a month for a spacious living room, bedroom, dressing room, kitchen, and dinette, with linens, maid, and complete hotel service. He spent a sleepless night thinking about what she had said. When he got up in the morning, he drew a floor plan of the suite in question, dividing it up into three spacious hotel rooms with baths. Calling in an architect, he explained his plan and asked for an estimate. When plans and estimate proved feasible, he ordered that the matching available apartments on floors 3 through 10 be converted to hotel rooms. Thus he increased the potential from six dollars a day to twenty-four dollars a day for the same space. The conversion was completed two weeks prior to Pearl Harbor, and the beginning of the country's biggest hotel boom. Counteracting his initial poor timing in building the Ponchartrain on the eve of the depression, Lysle Aschaffenburg had inadvertently launched his hotel on the crest of the wave that was to carry it on to ever-increasing success in the future.

At last able to buy out his partner, Mr. Williams (who made a handsome profit on his investment), Lysle Aschaffenburg was finally sole owner of the hotel he had built and struggled so hard to retain.

Now that the hotel was his, he was able to lavish his high standards and fine taste upon the rooms and suites. Not only are no two rooms identical but the remaining suites are decorated in the most exquisite fashion, with elegant antiques—mahogany and satinwood marquetry beds, an English Regency gilded chandelier, a Chinese Sung Celadon Temple vase mounted as a lamp. Each suite is furnished in a different style or period, each with an appropriate

Bayou Bar, Pontchartrain Hotel

name, and every one is done with loving care and no expense spared.

In 1947, Mr. Aschaffenburg had another of his "visions," as he calls them. Inspired by the example of Ernie Byfield, who *made* the Ambassador East in Chicago by creating the Pump Room, Lysle Aschaffenburg determined to do the same for the Pontchartrain. Horrified, his friends and family did everything they could to discourage him. Hazardous, impossible, they called it. How could he hope to compete with the famous French Quarter restaurants like Antoine's and Galatoire's some twenty blocks away? Undaunted, he countered that he was not building the restaurant for tourists. He felt the people of New Orleans would welcome a fine dining room with pleasant surroundings (there was none at that time), without the French Quarter tile floor and kitchen chairs, and without a dance band or floor show. He was right, but he was also wrong.

With delusions of creating another Pavillon, he imported chefs and a *maître d'hotel* as well as a decorator from New York. With educated hindsight he says today that he should have known better when he bragged to a wealthy New Orleanian at the country club that he was planning to have Continental service in his new dining room. "What's Continental service?" asked his friend, and in effect, "Who needs it?"

It was a dismal flop. It simply was not what the people of New Orleans wanted. So he fired all of his imported employees and brought back Thelma Walker, who had worked for him in the coffee shop. He put her in charge of personnel, and she hired a native chef who began producing the Creole and French food that New Orleanians appreciate. Almost immediately the Caribbean Room's popularity began to grow, and it is such a favorite of New Orleanians that they now make up 90 per cent of the capacity clientele. In fact, one local man told Mr. Aschaffenburg that he wasn't coming to eat there any more. "Why?" asked Mr. Aschaffenburg. "Did you get a tough steak?" "No," was the reply, "but I meet so many of my friends whenever I eat here that I get tired of jumping up and down to say hello."

Not only do New Orleanians enjoy seeing their friends when they dine out, but they feel more comfortable when the staff is familiar, and the Pontchartrain has been able to maintain great continuity in its personnel, with many employees of twenty to twenty-five years' standing.

However, it isn't only New Orleanians who enjoy the food at the Pontchartrain. People from out of town often phone saying they were told that they shouldn't leave without eating a meal there and having Mr. Aschaffenburg order it for them. Indeed, Mr. Aschaffenburg feels very strongly that when a host entertains in a restaurant, all of the ordering should be done in advance so that the whole meal can be planned and prepared properly. When a prospective host contests this theory, arguing that he can't tell whether his guests will want fish, meat, or fowl, Mr. Aschaffenburg then asks him what he'd do if he were inviting them to dinner in his home.

Judging from the almost legendary reports one hears of the fabulous private dinners that Mr. Aschaffenburg has planned for special occasions and celebrity visitors, such as Walt Disney, one could hardly do better than to entrust the menu to him. In fact, there's a story that Lysle Aschaffenburg issued a standing challenge—providing that guests let him select the food, there would be no check if they didn't agree it was one of the finest meals they had eaten in New Orleans!

It is obvious that the excellence of the food (and everything else about the Pontchartrain) is due to Lysle Aschaffenburg's passionate interest and devotion. As he explains it, his motivation is more pride than money. An ardent gourmet, Mr. Aschaffenburg is a member of numerous important international wine and food societies (he and Roy Alciatore of Antoine's head a distinguished group of citizens on the Grand Council of the New Orleans Chevaliers du Tastevin). He feels that a restaurant can be a fine one only if the owner knows good food, travels widely, and sets his standards high. He alone must be the arbiter of quality, and even if he is told that the customers like a dish a certain way, he will have it changed if he feels it is wrong. His son Albert, vice president and director of sales, who has fortunately inherited his father's fine taste and abilities, says that his father calls a meeting next day if he finds the French dressing isn't right. As a result of this infinite care for details, customers often phone their praise after eating there—and this is duly passed on to the cooks and waiters.

When the Pontchartrain gives a dinner for stage or screen celebrities, the menu is afterward added to the party menu repertoire and named after the celebrity for whom it was given. It isn't unusual for party-givers to pick a menu because it was served to Charles Laughton* or Mary Martin. Also, newly decorated suites are often named after celebrities who occupy them.

When Mary Martin first stayed at the hotel, her door was duly hung with a plaque christening it the Mary Martin Suite. Some years later, planning a return visit, she wired ahead to reserve the Mary Martin Suite. Meanwhile, in the course of the constant change and redecorating that takes place, her suite had been incorporated into another, which was occupied. However, before she arrived, the Aschaffenburgs had handsomely refurbished a new Mary Martin Suite, so that when she entered, she threw out her arms, exclaiming: "Oh, it's just as I remembered it!"

Charles Laughton left his mark on the Pontchartrain by chiding

* For the Charles Laughton Dinner, see the end of this chapter.

Charles Laughton Dinner

Crabmeat Remick

*

Shrimp Bisque
Sherry

*

Trout Véronique
Chablis
Parisienne Potatoes

*

Hot Rolls and Butter

*

Tossed Green Salad

*

Pot de Crème Vanille

*

Demitasse

Lysle Aschaffenburg for not incorporating the Garden District, which he preferred to the French Quarter, into the hotel's decor. Mr. Aschaffenburg forthwith commissioned Leonard Flettrich to paint murals for the coffee shop with a Garden District motif.

Many of the Pontchartrain's menu favorites have been contributed over the years by various members of the staff. Chef Nathaniel (Burt) Burton, trying to copy Antoine's Oysters Ellis, couldn't quite make it, and came up with Oysters Caribbean instead—creating one of the Pontchartrain's most popular dishes by accident. Trout Véronique was contributed by a *maître d'hotel*, and the famous Mile High Ice Cream Pie was the bequest of a short-lived pastry chef. Feeling they must have a really top-notch *patîssier*, the Aschaffenburgs hired this man from one of the hotels. After a short while he left—but not before his successors, Annie Laurie and Florence, learned to make the Ice Cream Pie!

Among other Pontchartrain traditions are Sunday and Wednesday buffet nights, and it is a custom on New Year's Day before the Sugar Bowl Game to have Chicken Hash and Grits Soufflé in the Caribbean Room.

According to Lysle Aschaffenburg, there is no business in which the dedication and good taste of the owner are so essential as they are in his. Lysle and his son Albert are fortunate in that they have the opportunity to give their unswerving dedication and abundant good taste free rein. They are grateful that they have no stockholders to answer to, so that they can plow the profits back into their hotel and restaurant. They say that the only thing that remains the same is the outside walls, so whenever people ask Lysle Aschaffenburg when the hotel was built, he answers, "Day before yesterday!"

Even as glamorous larger chain hotels rise in the city in growing numbers, the Pontchartrain remains the prestige address in New Orleans, and its Caribbean Room, now increased by twice in size and many times more in elegance, is one of *the* favorite restaurants in New Orleans.

Entrance to Patio, Commander's

Commander's Palace

Commander's Palace is an exceptionally fine restaurant in an old Victorian building in the middle of the Garden District. The quality of the food (which has won the *Holiday* Magazine Award annually since its inception) fills its many commodious dining rooms daily at lunch and dinner, in spite of the fact that it is some distance from the business section of the city.

The Garden District began as a suburb of New Orleans. Originally this area consisted of large plantations with stately homes facing the Mississippi River and fields of sugar cane and indigo extending far behind. The heart of the section where Commander's stands today was the great Livaudais Plantation. François de Livaudais, third-generation heir to the plantation, made a brilliant match with Céleste de Marigny, daughter of one of the wealthiest men in America. They were in the process of constructing a magnificent mansion on the Mississippi when their marriage broke up. She acquired the plantation as part of the settlement, and after departing to live in France as a marquise at the court of Louis Philippe, sold the land to real-estate developers. It was divided into streets and lots and put on the market.

This land, along with that of four other plantations was incorporated into the city of Lafayette in 1833; an independent municipality, with its own mayor and police, four miles from the city of New Orleans. The section of Lafayette City fronting on the river was the business district, a bustling port where cattle boats unloaded stock for a thriving slaughterhouse and its allied industries, tanners, soap- and candlemakers. Beyond the industrial center and bounded by what is now St. Charles Avenue was the residential section of the city of Lafayette, the Garden District. The New Orleans & Carrollton Railroad provided regular transportation up St. Charles Avenue from New Orleans to this rural suburban paradise, where flowers and foliage flourished in the rich silt brought down by an 1816 levee break. It became a popular site for the homes of wealthy "Americans"—the

Creoles, who snubbed the Americans invading their city after the Louisiana Purchase, had *their* homes in the French Quarter and on Esplanade Avenue.

In 1852 the city of Lafayette became part of the city of New Orleans. The Garden District, formerly a suburb, was now a residential section. Even more elegant homes were built in Greek Revival and Renaissance style, with broad galleries bordered in lacy wrought iron and surrounded by palm trees, sweet olives, magnolias, azaleas, and camellias. Jefferson Davis died in one of these houses, and George Washington Cable entertained Mark Twain in another.

In 1880, Émile Commander opened Commander's Palace at the corner of Washington Avenue and Coliseum Street. By the turn of the century its dining room was attracting gourmets, and it has continued to do so with remarkable consistency while passing through three different managements up to the present day. The Giarrantano family bought the restaurant from Émile Commander and ran it for twenty-five or thirty years until 1944, when their sons left the city to go into other professions. They sold it to Frank and Elinor Moran, who not only carried on the tradition of fine cuisine with the same chef and many of the same recipes, but expanded the menu with delightful new dishes, increased the size and scope of the business, and enhanced the charm of the surroundings with handsome interior decoration and the addition of the beautiful patio and gardens.

Mr. and Mrs. Moran had both been in the restaurant business before they met and married. Mrs. Moran's father was head bartender at Begué's, one of New Orleans' earliest and most colorful restaurants. She fondly recalls an old photograph of him adorned with a handlebar mustache, presiding over the bar in that famous establishment. Mr. Moran was brought up in San Antonio, the son of an Irish father and a Mexican mother. Leaving school in Mexico, he came to New Orleans at fifteen and went to work in the old Grunewald Hotel (now the Roosevelt) in the milk department. He worked his way up by the usual route: busboy, waiter, captain.

The Morans' first joint venture was a small neighborhood bar they bought in the Gentilly section of the city. They gradually began adding food to their business—on Friday nights they offered their customers all the shrimp and crabs they could eat with the purchase of (enormous) ten-cent steins of beer. Next addition to the menu was a fried chicken platter for twenty-five cents; then they added chili and roast beef. Mrs. Moran was the cook and Mr. Moran the bartender.

Patio, Commander's

Next the Morans bought a small restaurant on Esplanade Avenue near the French Quarter, which they ran successfully for several years. When their landlord raised the rent from sixty to three hundred dollars a month, they decided to buy Commander's from the Giarrantano family. At the beginning of the Morans' proprietorship in 1944, the restaurant consisted of two rooms and ten employees; now the capacity is quadrupled and there are 115 employees. The Morans lived in an apartment over the restaurant until Easter Sunday in 1948—four years after they took over the business. They had just received all their newly upholstered furniture from the decorator when a fire gutted the building, burning off the third floor entirely

and completely demolishing their living quarters. The inside of the restaurant had to be rebuilt, but the old Victorian stairs and woodwork on the second floor was salvaged, and, at the insistence of the customers and Mrs. Moran, so was the original bar. The exterior remained the same.

Mrs. Moran bought a sand lot next door to the restaurant in order to indulge her passion for gardening—and began filling it with grass, plants, and trees. Customers often went out to admire it, and they suggested putting tables outside. This is how the lovely patio evolved: the customers took over Mrs. Moran's garden. It is now a lush green show place, and Mrs. Moran has somehow found the time to buy and plant everything in it herself.

One could never think of the garden without its myna birds. The original myna bird, now almost a trademark of Commander's, was acquired quite by accident. The bird, Tajar, was brought from India by a serviceman who lived in the neighborhood. Learning that he was again being shipped overseas, he asked Mrs. Moran if she would like to buy the bird. He told her that Tajar could talk—indeed, had a repertoire of some fifty words. Mrs. Moran didn't believe the bird could talk, and had no idea what she would do with it, but she bought it because she thought the boy needed money. She was amazed when she heard Tajar perform. Not only did he have a fantastic vocabulary, but he did imitations in different voices, so she installed Tajar in the garden to entertain the guests. He was such a huge success that his fame began to spread. People came to Commander's from all over the country asking to see him, and he was even featured on television by "Candid Camera."

One Sunday in 1963 (it was either Easter or Mother's Day, Mrs. Moran recalls) a child striking the bars of the cage with a stick so frightened Tajar that he injured himself trying to escape, and went into a state of shock. Everyone told the Morans that the bird could not possibly be saved, so they bought a second myna bird to replace him. However, a veterinarian was found who dared undertake the fantastically delicate brain surgery needed to save him, and Tajar recovered. He is back in the garden again, but has never regained his memory. At first he didn't talk at all. Though he has now learned to speak again, he doesn't remember his own name, and even refuses to repeat it when it is spoken to him.

At night and in bad weather Mrs. Moran keeps the birds in her kitchen next door, where they talk incessantly. Customers from the restaurant have been known to knock at her door in the middle of the night asking to see them when they are not in the garden; and sometimes, when the Morans look out from an upstairs window, they see people looking up for hidden wires and microphones—they can't believe the conversation is being carried on between two birds.

At one time Mr. Moran considered opening another restaurant in the French Quarter, but decided instead to enlarge Commander's by using the second floor, which had been the Morans' apartment. There are now many beautifully redecorated rooms upstairs. The halls are done in wine-red embossed velvet and there are handsome

1880 Bar, Commander's

chandeliers and sconces, decorative pieces and prints, all selected by Mrs. Moran on shopping expeditions in New Orleans and New York on her few days off from the restaurant. Even the ladies' room is lovely, with a white marble tile floor, marble basin, and gold fixtures. The chandelier in the main dining room downstairs, one of a pair from a castle in France, is Baccarat crystal, with every prism stamped. The bronze herons in the patio pool came from Annie Laurie's castle in Scotland, and the unique chandelier in the bar was rescued from the demolition of the old Jewish Community Center on St. Charles Avenue. The patio used to have a marvelous floor made of multicolored pieces of marble collected from all over the city, but the surface proved to be dangerously slippery and unfortunately had to be covered with concrete and stone. To decorate the wall dividing the dining patio and the garden, Mrs. Moran hung empty wine bottles with interesting shapes. Customers began asking to have their own wine bottles hung there as they emptied them, with their names written on the labels, and sometimes the date as well if it was an important occasion. Now the wall is full of hanging bottles, and at night they make a handsome effect with lights shining through them from the garden behind. At Christmastime the garden is further enhanced with the decoration of two of its trees with ten thousand lights.

Mrs. Moran, a remarkable, self-effacing woman, is responsible for the handsome decor and the fabulous garden as well. She works in the restaurant every day, and most people think she is one of the hired help. She prefers it that way.

Despite the fame of the myna birds and the physical charm of the restaurant, the food, after all, is the thing; and Commander's is certainly unsurpassed in producing a fine meal.

Really unique at Commander's is their Soft Shell Turtle Stew; it is made at no other restaurant. The Morans inherited the recipe from the Giarrantanos and proceeded to make it famous. It creates quite a sizable problem for them, however, in keeping up the supply of soft-shell turtle, which is by no means easy to come by. The turtle that is used in Turtle Soup comes from the bayous, but soft-shell turtle is a sea turtle from the Florida coast. The Morans buy all the turtles they can get, their chief source being a man from Houma, Louisiana, who brings them down to the city live in a tank on his truck. Some weigh as much as two hundred pounds and are as big around as the restaurant tables, but the soft shell is often only a small part of the turtle.

Their noted Stuffed Flounder recipe was evolved some years ago before the days of deep freeze. Flounder, because it didn't keep for more than a day, was a drug on the market and therefore sold at ten or fifteen cents a pound, while other fish cost more than twice as much. Commander's decided to devise a recipe to utilize this fish that the fishermen couldn't sell. The Morans' Stuffed Flounder became very popular and much imitated, and is still one of their specialties, even though the price is no longer any object.

Shrimp Imperatrice was conceived to help promote the shrimp industry. The recipe was brought to Commander's by a representative of the shrimpers, and was changed by the chef to its present succulent form. The fluted border of mashed potatoes around the edge was

Main Dining Room, Commander's

originally added merely to keep the halved avocados from sliding around the plate, but it also serves to set the dish off to perfection.

Initially the Morans used an enormous menu, including every dish in their repertoire. As the restaurant grew in size, the menu had to be cut down, because they couldn't cope with such a short-order business on such a large scale. Mr. Moran plans the menus, changing the lunch menu daily and the dinner menu monthly (it has twelve entrees, however, so there is no lack of variety).

The chef, James Evans, has been in Commander's kitchen for thirty-six years, having started work for the Giarrantanos fifteen years before the Morans took over. Like most of the other fine New Orleans restaurants, Commander's has become a family affair. Mrs. Moran's son, Larry Grice, helps in the management and is in charge of the wines and liquors, and her grandson is starting at the bottom to work his way up from busboy and kitchen helper. Someone in the family is always on hand to make sure that things are running smoothly; and whoever it is never hesitates to pitch in at anything, from serving a drink to moving furniture in the patio when there is a sudden shower. No doubt this is one reason why Commander's has become so enormously successful entirely by word of mouth. The other reasons are apparent in their recipes, which will be found in the latter half of this book.

Le Médoc
EXIT
Paris

Masson's Beach House

Masson's Beach House differs from other New Orleans restaurants in at least two respects: its cuisine is French Provincial, influenced by the Creole only in its seasoning, and its location is far from the French Quarter and the Garden District—at West End. This area, bordering on Lake Ponchartrain, has changed so drastically in the days since Masson's Restaurant first began that it is virtually beyond recognition.

Yachtsmen and sailors of New Orleans anchor their boats around the elegant Southern Yacht Club at West End. Nearby, but certainly unrelated socially, is Bucktown, a small fishing village named after an old fisherman and hunter called Buck. Orleanians used to enjoy buying shrimp from the fishermen right out of their nets, and visitors still find it a great place to eat cold boiled crabs and shrimp while seated on benches at long wooden tables in ramshackle restaurants built on stilts out over the water. Bucktown, just outside Orleans Parish and therefore immune to its laws, has always been a sanctuary for all manner of illegitimate activities, such as speakeasies during Prohibition. Fun lovers from the city used to amuse themselves by visiting a couple of raffish little homosexual nightclubs with floor shows performed by female impersonators.

Not so many years ago there was a wide canal called the New Basin, running all the way out to West End from Carrollton Avenue. A narrow shell road bordered by swamp and trees alongside the canal gave rise to a common expression of the early twenties—"shell-roading." When the boys drove their dates out to the lake, it was said that if the girls didn't cooperate they dumped them out to walk home.

On Mardi Gras Day, King Zulu (the lively grass-skirted Negro-blackface spoof on Rex, the King of Carnival) used to sail down the New Basin Canal on a barge to the point where he alighted to be greeted by his followers and begin his parade.

Farther out on the lakefront was Spanish Fort, an early amuse-

Médoc Dining Room, Masson's

ment park, and Tranchina's, a nightclub and restaurant on a pier over the water. Piron, the crippled little Negro bandleader whose orchestra entertained nightly, wrote the popular song of the day, "I Wish I Could Shimmy Like My Sister Kate."

At West End there was a large successful hotel, and a park with a bandstand where concerts were held in the evening.

In those days there was no sea wall, and Mrs. Ernest Masson, Sr., recalls that after storms, everything flooded. The houses were built high off the ground, and everyone had to have his own little boat to get around in. Her mother kept chickens, ducks, and pigs and was forced to move them all onto the porch to save them from drowning each time the water rose.

It was here in 1915 that Albert Dubos, grandfather of Ernest and Albert Masson, built what is now Masson's Beach House. Albert Dubos came to New Orleans from France when he was twelve years old and went to work at Antoine's for founder Antoine Alciatore, as a kitchen helper and busboy. He was a contemporary and friend of Jules Alciatore's, the son and second proprietor of Antoine's. Dubos worked next for several years at the West End Hotel, a large and opulent resort that attracted guests from all over the country (in those days before air conditioning the lakefront was the place to go to cool off).

Albert Dubos, planning to return to France, was in New York City ready to embark when World War I broke out. Dubos went back to New Orleans, and in 1914 invested his savings and knowledge of the restaurant business in his own establishment at West End, calling it The Bungalow. He married a German girl and they ran the restaurant together. They were both excellent cooks. He taught her French cooking and she adapted to it so quickly that soon she was even better than he. One of Albert Dubos' recipes, which he called Toast Bungalow, is now the Canapé Maison at Masson's. Oysters Beach House is an adaptation of another of his recipes.

Dubos ran The Bungalow for about twenty-five years, until Mrs. Dubos died. Mr. Dubos then retired, closing his restaurant and renting the building. The first tenant was Chez Paree, a nightclub, in which Louis Armstrong and Louis Prima made their debuts. The Chez Paree, despite this auspicious contribution to the world of jazz, lasted only for six or seven years and was followed by a series of other tenants.

Albert Dubos' daughter had grown up in her father's restaurant.

After graduating from high school she went with her parents to France, where she took a course at the Cordon Bleu—"just for a lark." She remembers an uncle, a fine confectioner, who even at a very old age could still make a remarkably fine cake. Ernest Masson, whom she married, had been a pharmacist, but after retirement he suggested reopening the family restaurant. "Of course," she readily agreed. "That's what I've always wanted to do." So in 1945 The Bungalow began life anew, rechristened Masson's Beach House. It was an apt name because it was surrounded by water, with the canal in front and the lake behind.

The Massons had several fine French chefs. Mrs. Masson knew food by training and upbringing—and Mr. Masson was a good businessman—but it was their two sons, Ernest, Jr., and Albert, under whose management the restaurant gained its current fabulous reputation.

Both boys were Navy fliers. At the end of World War II, Ernest told his father that he wanted to come home and join his parents in the restaurant business. His father answered by telling him to "go to France and learn something about food."

Albert also decided that he wanted to return to the family business. His father told him to "go to France and learn something about wine."

Ernest made three trips to France. Twice he studied at the Cordon Bleu, and he feels that on the third trip he learned the most of all. He went with his mother and an uncle. They bought a car in Paris and toured the provinces, visiting his many cousins all over the country. A cousin in Paris had a café, and one in Roquefort had a *charcuterie*. Ernest feels that he learned many important things—things French housewives do in their cooking and specific dishes they made—that he feels mean more than those he learned in school. Then in Paris he was taken under the wing of Raymond Oliver, the chef of Le Grand Véfour. Oliver and the Massons became fast friends, and he taught Ernest a great deal. When *le maître* was here in America he came to visit the Massons often and was proud and pleased with the marvelous dishes his former student prepared—so much so that he awarded him a medal (a rare culinary honor) the Order of St. Fortunat.

When Ernest returned to his family's restaurant, he learned still more from Maurice, the chef at Masson's. Maurice was a skillful old Frenchman who directed his kitchen from a high stool, beside which he always kept his bottle of wine. He taught Ernest much of value that he hadn't learned in France—not the least of which was the operation of a restaurant kitchen and how to feed a hundred people as well as ten. From this sound background and experience, Ernest's natural talent as a chef bloomed and flowered, and his reputation spread by word of mouth to the point where his ability and prowess in the kitchen is most highly regarded by all the restaurant people and restaurant-goers of the extremely food-conscious city of New Orleans. The comparatively small and geographically far-out restaurant of rather humble beginnings began to attract customers from all over town, and international honors heaped upon him began to accumulate on the walls of the entrance and dining room.

Meanwhile Albert had followed his father's advice and studied the wine business. He went to Bordeaux and stayed as a guest for several months with the family of one of France's great vintners, Cruse et Fils. There could be no finer way to learn than living in the wine country with wine people. This was borne out some time later, when Albert was back in New Orleans running the restaurant with brother Ernest. Mr. and Mrs. Masson, Sr., were in France visiting the Cruses. M. Cruse told Mr. Masson about an unfortunate mistake that had been made in a shipment of wine from his vineyard to America. It seems that a special short cork has to be put in the bottles of wine intended for the American market, because the waiters have too much trouble removing the European corks. A shipment had gone out to America with long corks, and complaints were pouring in from all over the States: the customers didn't want the wine. M. Cruse showed Mr. Masson the wine and had him taste it. It was a marvelous wine—a beautiful wine. It was not expensive, and naturally there was bound to be a saving in rescuing this entire American shipment from deportation. Mr. Masson got on the phone at once to son Albert. "Don't worry, Papa," Albert told him. "I already have the wine—a whole warehouse full."

M. Cruse was highly amused. "I have your son for only a few months," he laughed, "and you see how well he has learned his lessons."

The Masson brothers took over the business in 1958, and their parents have gradually retired—giving place to more family in the business, Ernest's wife and a cousin. At first the restaurant attracted only local people. However, as the surroundings changed, so did their business. The concrete sea wall had been built some years earlier, and the formerly barren swampland around it was transformed into valuable real estate by filling it in with pumped sand. Named Lake Vista, this new suburb of a rapidly expanding city began to become fashionable and soon started burgeoning with new homes. The old shell road had long since given way to asphalt, and the New Basin Canal was filled in all the way to the yacht basin. With the enormous development of lakefront real estate and the new Causeway across Lake Ponchartrain came the ultramodern expressway from downtown New Orleans out to the lake, superseding the narrow asphalt that had replaced the old shell road. A brand-new Yacht Club rose where the old one had stood at West End. There is no longer a West End Hotel or a bandstand, but Bucktown and the cold-boiled-crab establishments are still there. Although Masson's Beach House was in a way left high and dry physically by the removal of the canal, it is now surrounded on all sides by many new customers, with a fast and easy route to its dining room from the city. And with Ernest's growing reputation for fine food and Albert's expertise in fine wines, New Orleans has beaten a path to their door.

*Lagniappe**

Although the purpose of this book is to cover the major New Orleans restaurants, there are many other places of interest concerned with eating and drinking that should not be left out.

Like most seaport towns, New Orleans is a melting pot, and all nationalities are well represented in its population, in spite of its French and Spanish origins. Although it may come as a surprise to many who think of the city as the home of Creole cuisine, there are also numerous fine Italian restaurants in New Orleans, such as Mosca's, Moran's, Pittari's, Sclafani's, Tortorici's, and Turci's.

A favorite with many New Orleanians is Manale's. Uptown, just off St. Charles Avenue, it attracts crowds of local people, who enjoy its accessibility and its good food, which has drawn rave reviews from national magazine columnists. The menu is primarily Italian, but chef Radosta (the restaurant has been in the hands of the Manale-Radosta family since it opened its doors in 1913) has a magic touch with seafood, and a few of his fine recipes are in this book.

Another chef whose work is represented is Nick Mosca, whose family owns Mosca's. After an apprenticeship with his father, Nick decided to go out on his own. He bought the beautiful Elmwood Plantation on the River Road above the Huey Long Bridge, and had the lovely and historic two-hundred-year-old house redecorated as a restaurant. It opened in 1961 and has since attracted crowds of admirers.

Among the older French Quarter restaurants is Broussard's. The founder was such an enthusiastic admirer of Napoleon that he installed two statues of his hero in the restaurant—one in the dining room and one in the courtyard. Whenever a guest orders a Napoleon brandy, a bell is rung in the garden and all the waiters salute the statue of Napoleon. Inside, when a dessert is flamed with cognac, a similar ceremony takes place, with the singing of "Madelon."

* Creole for "something extra."

There are many other very good small French restaurants (and a Viennese one as well, called Old Europe) that have their passionate *aficionados*—who will no doubt be enraged at their omission here, but no attempt can be made to include them all.

There are some interesting offshoots and side effects of the New Orleans food picture, not to be compared with the works of art served in the fine restaurants to be sure: the humble po' boy sandwich (a relative of the Italian "hero")—a split loaf of French bread piled high with sliced meats, cheeses, and tomatoes, available at corner groceries and delicatessens; the delicious oyster loaf, crisp fried oysters between French bread halves; the oyster bars serving oysters on the half shell, opened before your eyes as you wait to eat them. There is the shocker to Yankees, grits served with every order of bacon and eggs at Walgreen's drugstore on Canal Street—and the little street wagons dotted about the city offering hot tamales, so peppery that they are almost too fiery to eat without being drowned in catsup.

New Orleans coffee is something special unto itself. In the coffee-importing houses on Magazine Street the green coffee from Central and South America is roasted and blended by the expert "cuppers" before being shipped out to the rest of the country. Anyone who has ever tasted it knows that New Orleans coffee is unlike any other. Dripped very slowly in French coffeepots, it is always twice as strong as the ordinary American brew, and most New Orleanians prefer their coffee with chicory added (a leftover from post-Civil War days when it was used as a filler or substitute for scarce coffee) —which makes it even stronger.

The Four Seasons on Royal Street is a fine place to drink coffee with excellent pastries made on the premises. But the oldest and most popular coffeehouse is the Morning Call in the French Market. Opened in 1870 by Joseph Jurisich for the market people, it became a rendezvous where farmers, merchants, and clerks could pass on gossip during a coffee break. Later it began to attract the boatsmen and sportsmen from the river, and the stars and musicians from the French Opera House between rehearsals and after performances. Nearly a hundred years later it still serves this mixed clientele.

Only coffee and doughnuts are served at the Morning Call, but these doughnuts are worth traveling many miles to eat. More like a *beignet* or *zeppole* than a doughnut (and certainly unrelated to the heavy lump of dough with a hole in the middle that bears that name), these are hot, light, puffy golden squares with powdered sugar shaken over them. In the New Orleans tradition, Peter and Joseph Jurisich carried on father Joseph's business with the secret family recipe for doughnuts—kneaded and rolled on wooden slabs, cut into three-inch squares, and tossed into steaming kettles of hot fat.

The appearance of the Morning Call never changes. There are a few tables, but most of the seats are stools along marble counters where the coffee is served in thick white china cups and the sugar bowls are attached to the premises and one another by a long chain. (Curb service is also available.) In spite of the plainness of the service and the surroundings, debutantes and visiting celebrities rub elbows with truck drivers at the Morning Call—*the* place to wind up an evening in New Orleans, after Carnival ball, symphony concert, or a night on the town!

There is a story that the word "cocktail" originated in New Orleans. No one knows whether this is true, but there is no doubt about the origin of the Sazerac cocktail. The drink evolved from a concoction of New Orleans druggist Peychaud (the same alleged inventor of the cocktail), made of sugar, cognac, and bitters, and known as a brandy cocktail.

In 1859 the Sazerac Coffee House opened at 116 Royal Street. It took its name from the Sazerac Forge et Fils Brandy, imported from France by the proprietor, and the brandy cocktails made there became very popular. Although Peychaud's bitters remained in the drink, the brandy for which it was named was eventually replaced by rye whiskey. Another element of the Sazerac cocktail had to be changed when absinthe was banned in France and America, but absinthe substitutes were used in its stead without diminishing the potency or popularity of the Sazerac.

The Sazerac Coffee House became the Sazerac Bar, and then, during Prohibition, the Sazerac Restaurant. After Repeal, reviving from its enforced hibernation, it reopened at 300 Carondelet Street, where it attained enormous success with newspapermen, bankers, and businessmen. A daytime bar, it started its business at 9 A.M. for eye openers. The early shift from the newspaper came in at 3 P.M. From 4 to 5 P.M. there were free hot hors d'oeuvres for the cocktail hour, and the bar closed for the day at 8:30 in the evening. Women were allowed inside only on Mardi Gras Day—when all the wives came to see where their husbands had been spending their time and money. During the rest of the year ladies who came looking for their mates were obliged to wait seated on barrels in the freight entrance, where they sometimes had drinks sent out to them. The Sazerac had two cats, named after newsmen regulars, that drank beer from a saucer, and there was a Dutch priest who was considered the bar chaplain. Behind the bar was a mural painted by Xavier Gonzales, depicting all its habitués.

Sazerac became such a big business that the rights to it became the property of the Magnolia Liquor Company, which bottles the cocktail and controls the franchise. In 1949 the Roosevelt Hotel obtained the franchise and the Sazerac Bar was moved to the hotel, where ladies are now welcome at any time.

The Roosevelt Hotel also has exclusive rights for the Ramos Gin Fizz. This delightful drink was invented by Henry C. Ramos, who came to New Orleans in 1888 and operated a saloon in the same building at 300 Carondelet that was the second home of the Sazerac. Today the Roosevelt continues to pay a royalty to the Ramos family on every Gin Fizz it serves.

Another drink identified with New Orleans is the Hurricane, made famous by Pat O'Brien's French Quarter bar. Unlike the Sazerac and Gin Fizz, it was not invented here and is far from a secret. Pat O'Brien's prints the recipe on the back of all its cocktail napkins. Other houses can and do serve the Hurricane, but it has become practically synonymous with Pat O'Brien's, and nobody else is able to make a dent in the half a million a year O'Brien's sells. Walk down Canal Street or through the French Quarter at Mardi Gras and you will see the tall pink drink in its hurricane glass in every other hand. Wise to the fact that they would lose a fortune in glasses taken home as souvenirs, Pat O'Brien and partner Charlie Cantrell charge a dollar deposit on the glasses, which is repaid to those who give them back. However, half of them go home with the customers.

Not only is Pat O'Brien's the handsomest bar in New Orleans today (and probably unique anywhere for the loveliness of its courtyard) but when it opened at its present location in 1942, it was the only beautiful place in New Orleans for eating *or* drinking. Perhaps it started a trend, for now there are many, but at that time theirs was alone in looking the way one would expect New Orleans *should* look. The building goes back to 1791, and was said to have been a Spanish theater from 1807 to 1812. O'Brien and Cantrell bought it and remodeled it after running a successful (though dark and unbeautiful) bar a block away at 638 St. Peter Street since 1934 (after O'Brien came to town from Birmingham to spend the night, and never left). Inspired by the success of their Hurricane, they have invented a whole series of drinks with stormy names—the Squall, Cyclone, Breeze, etc., each with its distinctive glass—and they have given us the recipes for all of them, to try out in our homes.

RECIPES

FOLLOWING PAGES: *Southern Hospitality – Recipes*

Appetizers

BAKED CRABMEAT and AVOCADO

DUNBAR'S

1 stick butter · 2 cans cream of mushroom soup · 1 pound lump crabmeat · 1 cup evaporated milk · Salt and pepper to taste · 2 avocados · 2 tablespoons bread crumbs · Melted butter · 1 can anchovy fillets

Melt butter, add soup, and simmer 5 minutes. Stir in crabmeat, add milk, salt and pepper, and simmer 5 minutes longer. Peel and slice avocados. Line a baking dish with avocado slices and pour crabmeat mixture over avocado. Sprinkle with bread crumbs and brush with melted butter. Heat until brown, approximately 15 minutes, at 350°. Before serving sprinkle with a few drops of anchovy oil and garnish with anchovy strips.
Serves 4–6.

CRABMEAT CANAPÉ

ARNAUD'S

2 shallots (green onions), chopped very fine · 1/8 cup olive oil · 3 ounces medium cream sauce · 1/2 pound crabmeat · 1 ounce white wine · Salt and pepper · 1 teaspoon chopped parsley · 2 trimmed slices toast

Sauté shallots in oil. Blend in cream sauce, add crabmeat and wine, and season to taste. Cook about 8 minutes, sprinkle with parsley, and allow to cool. Spread on toast, bake in a moderate oven 5 minutes, and serve.
Serves 2.

CRABMEAT BIARRITZ

PONTCHARTRAIN

Shredded lettuce · 2 slices tomato, marinated in French dressing · 2 boiled artichoke hearts · 1 cup crabmeat, moistened with 1 tablespoon mayonnaise · 4 tablespoons mayonnaise · 2 tablespoons whipping cream · 2 teaspoons black caviar · 1 teaspoon capers

Place lettuce on serving plates, and on each place a slice of tomato and then an artichoke heart. Heap artichoke hearts with crabmeat that has been moistened with mayonnaise. Cover with a mixture of mayonnaise and whipping cream, top each with a spoonful of caviar, sprinkle with capers, and serve very cold.
Serves 2.

CRABMEAT BLANCHE

PONTCHARTRAIN

4 English muffins · ½ stick butter · 1 pound fresh mushrooms · 2 tablespoons butter · 1 pound fresh crabmeat · 2½ cups heavy cream sauce · Anchovy paste · 1 cup crumbled fresh bread

Split English muffins, toast lightly, and butter generously. Chop mushrooms and sauté lightly in butter for 5 minutes. Add crabmeat and mushrooms to cream sauce. Spread anchovy paste on muffins (very lightly) and pile crabmeat mixture on top. Sprinkle with

crumbs, dot with butter, and bake about 15 minutes at 350°. Can be prepared ahead of time and baked when ready to serve.
Serves 8 as appetizer, or 4 as main dish.

CRABMEAT LORENZO

COMMANDER'S

2 cloves garlic, chopped · 1 stick butter · ½ bunch shallots (green onions), chopped · 1 bell (green) pepper, chopped · 1 tablespoon flour · 1 cup milk · 6 sprigs parsley, chopped · ½ cup sherry · 1 pound crabmeat · 1 cup bread crumbs · Salt and pepper · 6 toast rounds · 12 anchovy strips · 4 tablespoons grated Parmesan cheese

Sauté garlic in butter until half browned. Add shallots and bell pepper. Cook slowly until done but not brown. Add flour and stir in well. Add milk and parsley, stirring until thick. Add sherry and fold in crabmeat. Sprinkle in bread crumbs, season to taste, and form into 6 balls. Lay each ball on a crisp toast round, and top each with 2 strips of anchovy. Sprinkle with grated Parmesan cheese and brown under broiler.
Serves 6.

CRABMEAT REMICK

PONTCHARTRAIN

1 pound lump crabmeat · 6 strips crisp bacon · 1 scant teaspoon dry mustard · ½ teaspoon paprika · ½ teaspoon celery salt · ½ teaspoon Tabasco sauce · ½ cup chili sauce · 1 teaspoon tarragon vinegar · 1½ cups mayonnaise

Divide crabmeat into 6 portions and pile into individual ramekins. Heat in oven and top with strips of crisp bacon. Blend together mustard, paprika, celery salt, and Tabasco sauce. Add chili sauce and vinegar, mix well, blend with mayonnaise. Spread the warm crabmeat with this sauce and glaze under the broiler flame.
Serves 6.

LA CHAIR DE CRABE À LA CREOLE
(Crabmeat St. Pierre)

ANTOINE'S

1½ pounds crabmeat · ¼ stick butter · ½ cup chopped shallots (green onions) · ¼ cup chopped bell (green) pepper · 1 cup peeled tomatoes · 1 clove minced garlic · 1 tablespoon chopped parsley · Salt and cayenne to taste · ½ cup bread crumbs · ½ cup grated Swiss cheese

Sauté crabmeat in butter only long enough to cook the meat. Add shallots, bell pepper, tomatoes, garlic, and parsley. Season to taste and cook all ingredients until slightly thickened. Cover with a mixture of bread crumbs and grated cheese. Pass under the broiler and serve immediately.
Serves 6.

OYSTERS ALBERT

MASSON'S

½ cup chopped shallots (green onions) · 2 sticks butter · Pinch each thyme, cayenne, garlic powder · ¼ cup bread crumbs · 2 teaspoons cognac · ⅛ cup white wine · 2 dozen raw oysters

Sauté green onions in butter with thyme, cayenne, and garlic powder. Cool. Remove half of this mixture, add crumbs and cognac, shape into roll, and refrigerate for several hours. Add white wine to remainder of butter-and-onion mixture. Add oysters and cook until their edges curl. Place 6 oysters in each serving dish and top each with a slice of refrigerated butter mixture. Bake 8–10 minutes at 350°.
Serves 4.

BAKED OYSTERS ON THE HALF SHELL

PONTCHARTRAIN

36 freshly opened oysters with shells · 9 strips bacon · 4 chopped shallots (green onions) · ½ stick butter · Salt and pepper to taste · 2 tablespoons butter · Juice of 1 lemon · 2 tablespoons chopped parsley

Have 6 piepans half filled with rock salt. Arrange 6 oysters on the

half shell in each. Top each oyster with a square of lightly broiled bacon. Sauté shallots in butter and season with salt and pepper (if oysters are not salty). Cover each oyster with an equal amount of this mixture and dot with butter. Melt 2 tablespoons butter, add lemon juice, and pour over oysters. Bake at 400° about 6 minutes, or until edges begin to curl. Garnish with chopped parsley.
Serves 6.

OYSTERS BEACH HOUSE

MASSON'S

¼ cup chopped shallots (green onions) · ¼ cup sliced mushrooms · 1 teaspoon dry mustard · Pinch cayenne · 1 stick butter · ¾ cup flour · 2 cups milk · ½ cup dry sherry · 2 egg yolks · 2 dozen raw oysters

Sauté shallots, mushrooms, mustard, and cayenne in butter. Add flour and cook 3–4 minutes. Add warm milk gradually, and cook 8–10 minutes. Add sherry. Remove from fire and stir in beaten egg yolks. Place room-temperature raw oysters in cleaned oyster shells and cover with sauce. Bake 10–12 minutes at 350°.
Serves 4.

OYSTERS BIENVILLE

ARNAUD'S

3 dozen oysters on the half shell, with oyster liquor · 1 bunch shallots (green onions) or 2 large yellow onions, chopped very fine · 1 stick butter · 2 heaping tablespoons flour · 1 pint chicken or fish broth · 1½ pounds boiled shrimp, cleaned and chopped very fine · 1 can mushrooms, chopped very fine · 3 egg yolks · ½ cup breakfast (light) cream or evaporated milk · 3 ounces white wine (sauterne type) · Salt, pepper, and cayenne or Tabasco · ¼ cup bread crumbs · ¼ cup grated Parmesan cheese · ⅛ teaspoon paprika

Have 6 piepans half filled with rock salt. Place 6 oysters in each pan and bake in a moderate (375–400°) oven about 10 minutes, or just until they curl around the edges. Remove and set aside.

Brown shallots or yellow onions in butter until they are golden, stirring constantly. Add flour, stirring over low flame until smooth and brown. Slowly add chicken or fish broth which has been heated to the scalding (not boiling) point. Add shrimp and mushrooms and simmer until mixture begins to thicken. Set aside and allow to cool slightly.

Beat egg yolks well with cream and wine. Then very slowly pour the warm sauce into the egg-cream-wine mixture, stirring and beating constantly to keep smooth and avoid curdling. Add liquor from oysters and then season to taste with salt, pepper, and a dash of cayenne or Tabasco sauce. Replace on fire and cook over low flame 10–15 minutes or until well thickened, stirring constantly. Add more flour if necessary. When the sauce is thick, spoon it carefully over individual oysters on the half shell and sprinkle each with a fairly thick covering of bread crumbs, grated cheese, and paprika mixed together. Bake at 400° until tops begin to turn golden brown. Serve at once.

Serves 6.

OYSTERS BIENVILLE

COMMANDER'S

⅛ pound bacon · 4 ounces sliced mushrooms · 4 cloves garlic, chopped · ¼ bunch shallots (green onions), chopped · ½ stick butter · 2 cups flour · 1½ quarts milk · ¼ teaspoon egg-shade food coloring · ½ pound boiled shrimp, diced small · ½ pint oyster juice · ½ cup lemon juice · ½ cup sherry · ¼ cup chopped parsley · 6 dozen oysters with shells

Cut bacon into small pieces and fry until brown. Sauté mushrooms, garlic, and shallots. Add butter and when it has melted, blend in flour. Cook slowly 5 minutes, then gradually stir in milk. After sauce thickens add egg coloring, shrimp, oyster juice, lemon juice, sherry, and parsley. Simmer slowly 15 minutes.

Have 12 piepans half filled with rock salt. Arrange 6 oyster shells in each piepan. Put a raw oyster (at room temperature) on each shell and top with sauce. Place under broiler (6 inches from flame) until heated thoroughly and browned on top.

Serves 12.

OYSTERS BROCHETTE

ANTOINE'S

10 slices bacon · 36 raw oysters · Seasoned flour · ⅔ cup butter · ⅓ cup olive oil · 12 toast triangles · 1 teaspoon chopped parsley · 1 teaspoon lemon juice

Cut bacon into 1-inch pieces and fry until partially cooked on both sides, draining off fat. On each of 6 skewers string 6 pieces of bacon alternated with 6 oysters, sticking the skewer through the eye of the oyster. Roll in flour. Heat butter and oil in a skillet and sauté skewered oysters and bacon, turning to cook all sides. Lay each skewer on 2 trimmed toast triangles. Add parsley and lemon juice to butter and oil remaining in skillet, and pour a little over each portion.
Serves 6.

OYSTERS CARIBBEAN

PONTCHARTRAIN

½ stick butter · 3 chopped shallots (green onions) · 1 quart oysters, drained · 2 cups medium cream sauce · ½ cup beef stock · 1 teaspoon chopped parsley · 2 teaspoons Worcestershire sauce

Sauté shallots in butter. Brown oysters on a heavy grill (or if this is not feasible, brown oysters dry in a heavy iron skillet until they form a crust on each side) and add to shallots in saucepan. Sauté slowly for 5 minutes, then add other ingredients. Simmer 5 minutes and serve in individual ramekins.
Serves 8.
Can be served as an entree in larger casserole dishes with a mound of steamed rice in the center of each serving.
Serves 4.

OYSTERS CARNAVAL

DUNBAR'S

2 dozen oysters with shells and liquid · 1½ large or 2 small onions · 1 small clove garlic · ½ bay leaf · 2 pieces celery · Pinch of thyme · 3 tablespoons butter · ½ cup bread crumbs · 2 tablespoons butter · ¼ cup bread crumbs · 2 tablespoons butter · 6 strips bacon · 6 lemon wedges

Chop oysters and drain, reserving liquid. Mince onions, garlic, bay leaf, celery, and thyme. Fry until brown in an iron skillet in 3 tablespoons of butter. Add chopped oysters. Moisten ½ cup bread crumbs with oyster liquid and add to mixture in skillet. Simmer for about 20–30 minutes, or until oysters have stopped drawing water. Add 2 tablespoons butter and cook until butter is melted. Boil and scrub oyster shells and fill with oyster mixture. Sprinkle with bread crumbs and dot with butter. Put in a 375° oven a few minutes until thoroughly heated. Serve at once, garnished with crisp bacon strips and lemon wedges.
Serves 6.

DEVILED OYSTERS ON THE HALF SHELL

PONTCHARTRAIN

14 oysters in shells · 2 tablespoons finely chopped shallots (green onions) · 1 tablespoon butter · 2 tablespoons flour · ½ teaspoon salt · ⅛ teaspoon nutmeg · Dash cayenne · 1 tablespoon Worcestershire sauce · ½ teaspoon chopped parsley · ½ teaspoon prepared mustard · 1 (3-ounce) can mushrooms, drained and chopped · 1 slightly beaten egg yolk · ½ cup cracker crumbs · 1 tablespoon melted butter

Remove oysters from shells, reserving ⅓ cup liquid, and wash and chop. Wash shells. Sauté shallots in butter, blend in flour, and brown. Stir in oyster liquid, salt, nutmeg, cayenne, Worcestershire sauce, parsley, mustard, and mushrooms. Add oysters and cook 3 minutes, stirring constantly. Remove from heat and add egg yolk. Arrange oyster shells in 2 piepans half filled with rock salt. Fill oyster shells

and sprinkle with a mixture of crumbs and melted butter. Bake about 10 minutes at 350°.
Serves 2.

OYSTERS DIABLO

PONTCHARTRAIN

3 dozen oysters with shells · 3 finely chopped shallots (green onions) · ½ cup finely chopped celery · 1 small can chopped mushrooms · 1 tablespoon butter · Few grains cayenne · ½ teaspoon salt · ½ teaspoon prepared mustard · 1 teaspoon dry mustard · 1 tablespoon Worcestershire sauce · ½ teaspoon chopped parsley · 4 slices stale French bread, squeezed out in water and chopped fine · 2 beaten egg yolks · Bread crumbs · Butter

Wash and chop oysters. Cook shallots, celery, and mushrooms in butter. Add oysters and cook until half of liquid is reduced. Add all seasonings and bread, mix well, and cook 3–4 minutes. Remove from fire and stir in egg yolks, mixing well again. Arrange 6 oyster shells in each of 6 piepans half filled with rock salt, fill each shell with oyster mixture, cover with crumbs, dot with butter, and bake 8–10 minutes at 400°.
Serves 6.

OYSTERS HOLIDAY

BRENNAN'S

1 pound diced bacon · 2 tablespoons finely chopped garlic · 3 bunches shallots, (green onions) chopped · 3 green peppers, chopped · 1 cup strained turtle soup · ½ cup finely chopped parsley · 1 (#3) can pimentos, chopped · Tabasco sauce · Salt and pepper · Worcestershire sauce · 3 dozen large oysters

Fry the bacon, but do not drain. Add garlic, shallots, and green pepper to the bacon and cook for a few minutes. Add turtle soup, parsley, and pimentos and season with Tabasco sauce, salt, pepper, and Worcestershire sauce.
Have 6 piepans half filled with rock salt. Place 6 oysters in each pie-

pan and bake until the edges begin to curl. Remove from oven and cover each oyster with the sauce. Serve immediately.
Serves 6.

OYSTERS KIRKPATRICK

COMMANDER'S

6 raw oysters on half shell · 6 teaspoons chili sauce · ½ teaspoon grated Parmesan cheese · 6 (1-inch) squares bacon

Arrange oysters on the half shell on a bed of rock salt in a pie-pan. Combine chili sauce and grated cheese. Cover each oyster with 1 teaspoon of the mixture and top with bacon. Bake 8 minutes at 400°.
Serves 1.

OYSTERS ROCKEFELLER

COMMANDER'S

8 ounces finely chopped bacon · 6 cloves garlic, chopped · 1 stick butter · 1 bunch shallots (green onions), finely chopped · 6 cups finely chopped canned or cooked spinach with juice · 1 bunch parsley, chopped fine · 1 tablespoon celery salt · ¼ teaspoon cayenne pepper · 1 cup oyster liquid · 4 ounces absinthe · Salt to taste · Bread crumbs · 6 dozen oysters with shells

Brown bacon, add garlic, and nearly brown. Add butter and shallots and after cooking a few minutes, add spinach and all other ingre-

dients. Thicken with bread crumbs and simmer 10 minutes.
Have 12 piepans half filled with rock salt. Arrange 6 oyster shells in each piepan. Top each oyster (at room temperature) in its shell with the sauce, and put under broiler 6 inches from flame until heated through and browned on top.
Serves 12.

OYSTERS ROCKEFELLER

GALATOIRE'S

1 stalk green celery · ½ pound spinach · 1 bunch regular celery · 1 bunch shallots (green onions) · 1 bunch anise · 1 bunch parsley · 6 sticks butter · 2 ounces Lea & Perrins Sauce · 1 ounce absinthe · Salt, pepper, and cayenne · 4 dozen oysters

Wash vegetables well and grind very fine. Melt butter and add vegetables. Add Lea & Perrins Sauce and absinthe and season to taste. Have 8 piepans half filled with rock salt. Arrange 6 oysters (at room temperature) on the half shell on the bed of rock salt in each piepan. Cover each oyster with vegetable mixture and place under broiler until heated through. Serve at once.
Serves 8.

OYSTERS ROFFIGNAC

BRENNAN'S

1½ sticks butter · ⅓ cup finely chopped mushrooms · ⅓ cup finely chopped shallots (green onions) · ½ cup finely chopped onion · ½ cup finely chopped boiled shrimp · 2 tablespoons minced garlic · 2 tablespoons flour · ½ teaspoon salt · ⅛ teaspoon pepper · Dash cayenne · 1 cup oyster water · ½ cup red wine · 2 dozen oysters

Lightly sauté in butter mushrooms, shallots, onion, shrimp, and garlic. When onion is golden brown, add flour, salt, pepper, and cayenne. Brown well, about 7–10 minutes. Blend in oyster water and wine and simmer 15–20 minutes. Preheat in oven 4 piepans half filled with rock salt. Arrange 6 oysters (at room temperature)

on the half shell in each piepan and cover each oyster with stuffing, preferably with a pastry tube. Bake at 400° 10–12 minutes, or until oyster edges begin to curl.
Serves 4.

OYSTERS SUZETTE

ARNAUD'S

½ bell (green) pepper, chopped fine · 2 slices raw bacon, chopped fine · ½ pimento, chopped fine · 1 tablespoon olive oil · 1 dozen oysters on the half shell

Parboil bell pepper 5 minutes. Sauté bacon lightly, then add chopped bell pepper and pimento. Add oil and simmer about 5 minutes. Have 2 piepans half filled with rock salt. Arrange 6 oysters (at room temperature) in each pan of rock salt and bake about 20 minutes in a very slow oven. Cover each oyster with bacon-pepper-pimento mixture. Run under broiler 5–6 minutes and serve.
Serves 2.

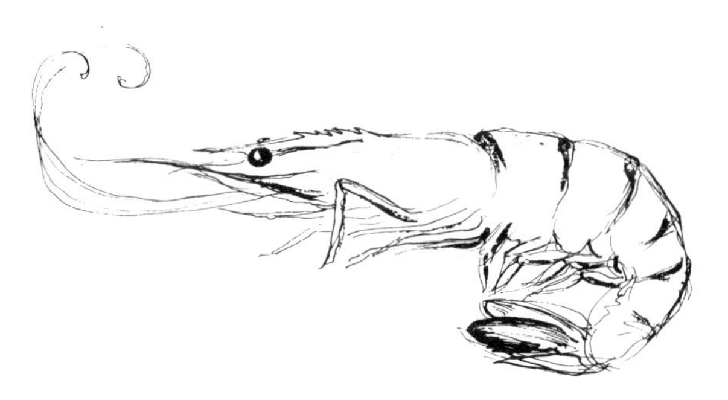

CREVETTES À L'AMÉRICAINE

BRENNAN'S

12 raw shrimp · 1 tablespoon butter · 1 tablespoon finely chopped onion · 1 ounce brandy · ½ cup velouté de poisson (cream sauce made with fish stock) · ½ tablespoon tomato purée · Cayenne, salt, and pepper to taste

Sauté shrimp in butter with onion. Add brandy and velouté de poisson, tomato purée, and seasoning.
Serves 1.

SHRIMP CANAPÉ À LA IRMA

ARNAUD'S

1 bunch shallots (green onions), minced · 1 clove garlic, minced · 2 tablespoons butter · 2 tablespoons flour · Fish broth (about 1 cup) · 2 pounds boiled shrimp · 1 cup claret · 1 cup white wine · 4 egg yolks · 8 slices toast · Bread Crumbs · Grated Parmesan cheese

Sauté shallots and garlic in butter until brown. Make a roux with flour, shallots, and garlic and add fish broth to thickness desired. Slice shrimp fine and add to sauce. Cook about 20 minutes. Add claret, and white wine mixed with egg yolks. Spread on slices of trimmed toast, sprinkle with crumbs and grated cheese, and bake until golden brown.
Serves 8.

SHRIMP DIJON

BRENNAN'S

2 tablespoons finely chopped shallots (green onions) · 1 teaspoon minced garlic · 1 teaspoon butter · Pinch of thyme · Pinch of basil · 1 cup white wine · Salt and pepper to taste · 2 cups bread crumbs · 12 medium-sized boiled shrimp · 1 ounce sherry

Sauté onions and garlic in butter. Add thyme, basil, wine, salt and pepper. Mix in bread crumbs and cook 5–10 minutes. Transfer to a pan to cool in refrigerator. To serve, put 6 shrimp in each individual serving dish and cover with reheated mixture, sprinkle with bread crumbs and sherry.
Serves 2.

SHRIMP MADELEINE

PONTCHARTRAIN

1 dozen raw shrimp, peeled and cleaned · ½ stick butter · 1 tablespoon chopped shallots (green onions) · 1 tablespoon chopped celery · 1 tablespoon chopped bell (green) peppers · 1 tablespoon chopped parsley · 2 tablespoons lemon juice · 1 teaspoon Worcestershire sauce

Sauté all ingredients except shrimp 3–4 minutes. Add shrimp and cook 5–6 minutes.
Serves 2.

SHRIMP MARINIÈRE

ANTOINE'S

1½ pounds raw shrimp · 2 cups white wine · 2 minced shallots (green onions) or ¼ cup minced onion · 1 cup oyster water, fish stock, or chicken stock · 2 tablespoons butter · 2 tablespoons flour · Juice of ¼ lemon · 2 egg yolks · ½ cup light cream · 1 tablespoon chopped parsley

Peel and devein shrimp. Combine wine, shallots, and oyster water, bring to a boil, and add shrimp. Simmer about 15 minutes. Melt butter and blend in flour. Gradually add ¾ cup of the wine-oyster water in which the shrimp were cooked, stirring constantly until thickened. Add shrimp and cook 10 minutes, then add lemon juice. Beat egg yolks and mix with cream. Combine with hot shrimp mixture, stirring constantly. Serve on toast points or in ramekins garnished with parsley.
Serves 6.

SHRIMP MARINIÈRE

COMMANDER'S

1 pound peeled raw shrimp · ½ stick butter · 1 chopped shallot (green onion) · 2 teaspoons flour · 1 cup fish broth · 2 tablespoons sliced mushrooms · ½ teaspoon chives · 1 teaspoon chopped parsley · 2 ounces dry sauterne · Salt and pepper to taste · Bread crumbs

Sauté shrimp in butter, add shallot, and continue cooking about 2 minutes. Blend in flour and gradually stir in fish broth. Add all other ingredients except bread crumbs. Simmer 5 minutes, pour into a casserole, sprinkle with crumbs, and brown in hot oven or under broiler.
Serves 4.

SHRIMP MOSCA

ELMWOOD

2 pounds shrimp in shells, headless · 2 bay leaves · Pinch oregano · Pinch rosemary · Pinch fresh ground pepper · 1 teaspoon salt · 5 or 6 pods garlic · 1½ ounces olive oil · 1 ounce sauterne

Place all ingredients in a skillet and sauté over hot fire 15–20 minutes, stirring occasionally, until shrimp are slightly brown. Add sauterne and cook over lower heat about 10 minutes, or until wine evaporates. Serve in shells—followed by finger bowls.
Serves 4.

SHRIMP SAKI

PONTCHARTRAIN

1 pound shrimp, cleaned and peeled · Salt and pepper · Paprika · 2 tablespoons lemon juice · ⅓ cup melted butter

Split shrimp down the back and place on a baking sheet. Season with salt and pepper and sprinkle with paprika. Bake 8 minutes at 425°. Place under broiler 5 minutes. Combine lemon juice and butter and serve with shrimp.
Serves 4–6.

ARTICHOKE HEART MORNAY

PONTCHARTRAIN

1 tablespoon very finely chopped ham · 1 tablespoon very finely chopped mushrooms · 2 slices truffles, chopped fine · ⅛ cup Béchamel sauce · 1 large artichoke heart (cooked in water seasoned with salt and lemon) · ⅛ cup Mornay sauce

Mix ham, mushrooms, and truffles with Béchamel sauce and pile into artichoke heart in a small individual ramekin. Cover with Mornay sauce and broil a few minutes just before serving.
Serves 1.

HEART OF ARTICHOKE EN SURPRISE

ARNAUD'S

5 ounces crabmeat · 1 shallot (green onion), chopped very fine · 1 piece celery, chopped very fine · 2 teaspoons mayonnaise · ½ tablespoon vinegar · Salt and white pepper · 2 artichoke hearts

Mix crabmeat with shallot, celery, mayonnaise, and vinegar and season to taste. Pile on artichoke hearts and serve, topped with mayonnaise, on lettuce leaves.
Serves 2.

HEART OF ARTICHOKE VERSAILLES

PONTCHARTRAIN

3 large artichokes · 3 or 4 lemon slices · 3 (½-inch-thick) tomato slices · ½ cup French dressing · 6 grated hard-boiled eggs · ⅓ cup mayonnaise · ½ teaspoon salt · Dash pepper · 3 teaspoons caviar · Thousand Island dressing

Cut 1 inch off tops of artichokes and cook in salted water with lemon slices 25–30 minutes, or until a leaf pulls out easily. Drain and remove leaves and choke. Chill hearts and tomato slices in French dressing at least 1 hour. Combine eggs, mayonnaise, salt, and pepper and chill. Place tomato slices on lettuce, cover with artichoke hearts, and pile each heart with egg salad. Top each with a teaspoon of caviar. Pass Thousand Island dressing.
Serves 3.

AVOCADO ROMANOFF

ARNAUD'S

½ pound crabmeat · 4 teaspoons mayonnaise · 2 pieces celery, chopped very fine · 2 shallots, (green onions), chopped very fine · 1 tablespoon vinegar · Salt and white pepper · 1 avocado · 2 tablespoons caviar

Mix crabmeat with mayonnaise, celery, shallots, and vinegar and season to taste. Cut avocado in half, place each half on a lettuce leaf, pile with crabmeat, and top each with 1 tablespoon of caviar. Serves 2.

CANAPÉ MAISON

MASSON'S

WHITE SAUCE: *3 sticks butter · 1 cup flour · 2 cups hot milk · Salt and pepper*

½ cup chopped shallots (green onions) · 1 clove garlic, chopped · 1 pound cooked crabmeat · ⅛ teaspoon cayenne pepper · 1 pint heavy white sauce · 4 trimmed slices toast · ¾ cup grated Cheddar cheese

To make white sauce: Melt 2 sticks butter in a heavy-bottomed pot. Add flour and simmer (do not brown) 5–6 minutes, stirring constantly as milk is added. Season to taste.
Sauté shallots and garlic in remaining butter. Add crabmeat and pepper and cook 4–5 minutes. Add white sauce and cook 5–8 minutes. Cool until fairly firm. Spread on toast and cover with grated cheese and bake at 350° 6–8 minutes, or until cheese melts.
Serves 4–6.

LOBSTER MARINADE

MASSON'S

1 clove garlic · 2 teaspoons salt · ¼ teaspoon pepper · ¼ cup wine vinegar · 1 cup olive oil · ½ cup chopped shallots (green onions) · 2 tablespoons chopped parsley · 1 pound cooked lobster meat

Mash garlic in a wooden bowl with salt and pepper. Add vinegar and mix well. Add oil, shallots, and parsley. Mix well. Pour over lobster meat and toss lightly. Refrigerate 2–3 hours before serving. Serves 4–6.

GRILLED GRAPEFRUIT

BRENNAN'S

1 large grapefruit, halved · 4 tablespoons sugar · 2 ounces kirschwasser · 2 maraschino cherries · 4 mint sprigs

Prepare grapefruit by removing core and loosening meat from skin. Sprinkle top generously with sugar and then kirschwasser. Broil 2–3 minutes, or until top starts to brown. Garnish with cherries and mint sprigs.
Serves 2.

FRESH MUSHROOMS SOUS CLOCHE

ANTOINE'S

1 pound fresh mushrooms · 3 tablespoons butter · 1 cup water · ½ cup white wine · 1 tablespoon flour · Juice of ½ lemon · 1 egg yolk · ¼ cup breakfast (light) cream · 4 slices toast

Wash mushrooms well. Melt 1 tablespoon butter and stir in water and wine. Add mushrooms, bring to boiling point, cover, and simmer 10 minutes. Drain, reserving liquid. Melt 2 tablespoons butter, blend in flour, add liquid in which mushrooms were cooked, and simmer, stirring constantly, until slightly thickened. Thinly slice mushrooms and add to sauce with lemon juice. Cook 5 minutes. Beat egg yolk and add to cream. Gradually add to mushroom mixture, mixing well. Divide into 4 servings and pour each into a heated glass bell, sealing bottom of bell with round of toast cut to fit. Turn bell over into a shirred-egg dish and serve immediately. Remove bell at table, or serve on toast without bell if desired.
Serves 4.

QUICHE LORRAINE

MASSON'S

1 (9-inch-diameter, 2-inch-deep) pie shell · 3 eggs · 1½ cups heavy cream · 1 teaspoon flour · Salt and pepper · 3 ounces thin-sliced Swiss cheese · ½ pound partially cooked chopped bacon

Partially bake pie shell. Beat eggs and combine with cream. Add

flour and salt and pepper. Arrange slices of cheese on bottom of pie shell and cover with bacon. Pour egg-and-cream mixture over bacon and cheese slowly. Bake at 350° 30–40 minutes, or until cake tester comes out clean.
Serves 6–8.

TARTELETTES AU FROMAGE

ANTOINE'S

3 eggs · 2 cups breakfast (light) cream · Salt and pepper · 1 cup grated Swiss cheese · 1 tablespoon melted butter · 12 partially cooked piecrust tart shells · ⅔ cup diced Swiss cheese

Beat eggs and cream together and season to taste. Add grated cheese and melted butter. In the bottom of each (¾-cooked) tart shell, put a spoonful of diced cheese. Then fill shell with custard mixture and bake at 350° about 15 minutes, or until custard is set or slightly browned.
Serves 12.

Soups

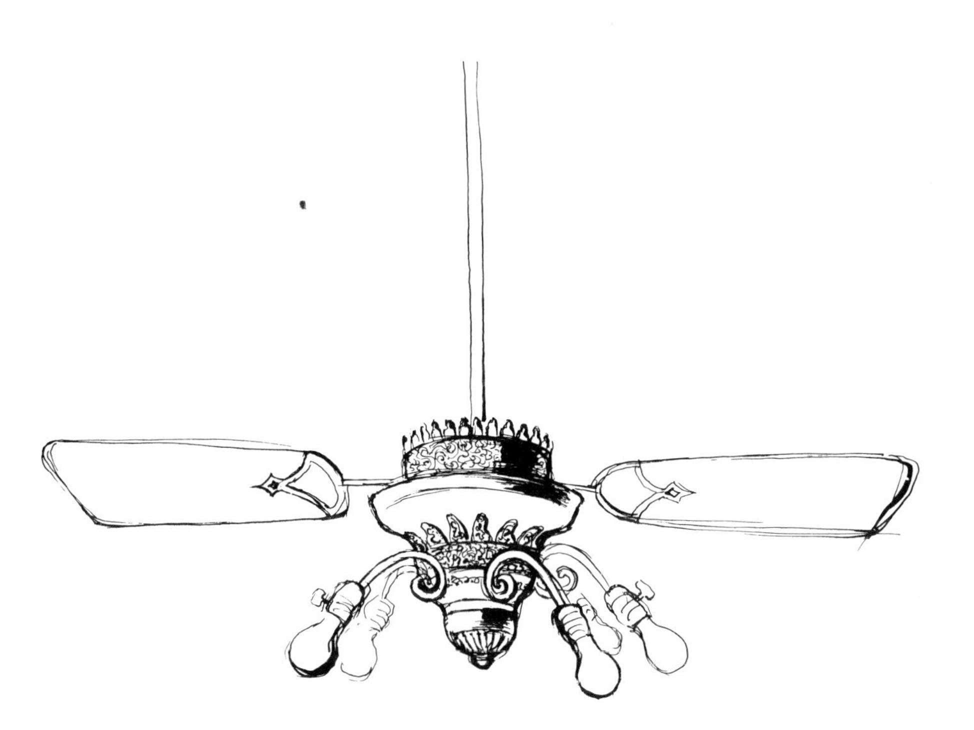

CRAWFISH BISQUE

DUNBAR'S

SOUP: *2 pounds crawfish · 1 pound shrimp · 3 quarts water · 1½ medium-sized onions · ¾ clove garlic · 2 pieces celery · 4 sprigs thyme · 2 bay leaves · 2 cloves (optional) · 3 ounces tomato paste · ½ cup flour · ¼ cup water · 1 teaspoon Kitchen Bouquet*

STUFFING: *2 tablespoons shortening · ½ onion · ¼ clove garlic · 1 piece celery · 2 sprigs thyme · ⅛ cup tomato paste · Salt, pepper, and cayenne · ½ loaf French bread*

Soak crawfish 1 hour in strong salted water. Drain, rinse, and drain again. Boil shrimp a few minutes in 1 quart lightly salted water.

Remove shrimp, peel, and finely chop. Reserve for stuffing. Put shrimp heads back in water in which shrimp were boiled, add 2 more quarts of water and crawfish. Add onions, garlic, celery, thyme, bay leaves, cloves, and tomato paste. Boil about 30–40 minutes, remove crawfish, and strain broth. Add flour-and-water mixture to broth for thickening, and Kitchen Bouquet. Simmer 2 hours, stirring frequently.

To make stuffing: Peel crawfish, saving heads, and chop fine. Combine with chopped shrimp. Simmer about 30 minutes in shortening together with onion, garlic, celery, thyme, and tomato paste. Break up French bread into small pieces, squeeze out after soaking in water, and add to crawfish, shrimp, and seasonings. Simmer about 20 minutes longer, stirring constantly. Let cool, then stuff into the empty shells of crawfish heads. Before serving, stuffed heads may be browned slightly in moderate oven. Add 3 or 4 heads to each bowl of soup.
Serves 10.

GUMBO FILÉ

DUNBAR'S

1 pound shrimp · 2 quarts water · 1 small onion, minced · 1 clove garlic, minced · 2 teaspoons shortening · 2 pieces celery, chopped · 1 bay leaf · 2 sprigs parsley, chopped · 2 sprigs thyme, chopped · 1 tablespoon Worcestershire sauce · 1 cup flour · ½ cup water · Salt and pepper to taste · 1 pint oysters · 1 tablespoon filé powder

Shell shrimp and boil shells 10 minutes. Save water, adding enough to make 2 quarts. Reserve shrimp and shrimp stock. Brown onion and garlic in shortening, then add celery, bay leaf, parsley, thyme, and Worcestershire sauce. Add this mixture to shrimp stock. Thicken with flour-and-water mixture and season with salt and pepper. Boil slowly about 1 hour. Add oysters and shrimp and cook until oysters curl. Add filé powder just before serving, stirring while sprinkling into gumbo.
Serves 10.

CREAM OF ARTICHOKE SOUP

MASSON'S

½ cup chopped shallots (green onions) · 1 piece celery, chopped · 1 medium-sized carrot, chopped · 1 bay leaf · Pinch of thyme · ½ stick butter · 1 quart chicken consommé · 1 cup sliced cooked artichoke hearts · 2 egg yolks · 1 cup heavy cream · Salt and pepper

Sauté shallots, celery, carrot, bay leaf, and thyme in butter. Add consommé and simmer 10–15 minutes. Add artichoke hearts and simmer 5–10 minutes. Remove from fire and add beaten egg yolks mixed with cream. Season to taste.
Yields 1½–1¾ quarts.

OKRA, CRAB, AND SHRIMP GUMBO

ANTOINE'S

6 heavy crabs · 1 pound medium-sized shrimp · 2 pounds selected okra · 2 kitchen spoons shortening · 1 level kitchen spoon flour · 3 large onions, chopped fine · 1 small can tomato paste · Salt to taste · 3 large bay leaves · 2 sprigs thyme · ½ teaspoon Tabasco sauce · 1 medium-sized can peeled tomatoes · 2 quarts water · 1 tablespoon Lea & Perrins Sauce

Scald and clean crabs, saving all the fat. Remove claws and cut bodies in half. Clean and shell shrimp but do not cook. Wash and thoroughly dry okra. Slice in thin discs. Fry in black iron skillet, stirring all the while so as not to scorch. Drain off all excess fat. In another pan make a roux with fat and flour, cooking until light brown. Add onions and sauté until soft. Add tomato paste, cooking and stirring until well blended. Remove all excess fat and stir in salt, crunched bay leaves, thyme, and Tabasco sauce. Blend well and then add the peeled tomatoes, cooking slowly until the whole mixture is uniform and a dark rich color. Now add the fried okra and 2 quarts of water, a little at a time. When bubbling again, add crab claws and bodies and any fat of crabs. Cook a while and then add the raw shrimp. Cover pot and allow to simmer gently at

least another hour. Taste for seasoning and add the Lea & Perrins Sauce before serving. Serve in a soup plate with a mound of cooked long-grain rice.
Serves 8.

SEAFOOD GUMBO

COMMANDER'S

6 tablespoons flour · ½ cup shortening · 6 cloves garlic, chopped · ½ cup diced onion · ¼ cup chopped bell (green) pepper · ½ cup chopped celery · 2 pounds peeled raw shrimp · 1 (8-ounce) can tomato sauce · 3 quarts water · 1 pound claw crabmeat · ¼ bunch chopped parsley · ½ teaspoon thyme · 3 bay leaves · 1 can or 1 package frozen okra · ½ pint oysters with juice · Salt and pepper to taste

Make a roux with flour and shortening. Add garlic and cook until golden brown. Add onion, bell pepper, and celery and cook until transparent. Add shrimp and tomato sauce, simmer 10 minutes, stir in water, and blend well. Add all other ingredients except okra and oysters. Cook 1 hour, add okra, and cook 20 minutes. Add oysters and cook 10 minutes longer. Serve in a soup bowl over steamed rice.
Yield: 1 gallon.

SEAFOOD-OKRA GUMBO

DUNBAR'S

1½ pounds fresh okra · Shortening · 1 small onion, ground · 1 clove garlic · ¼ can tomatoes · ¼ can tomato paste · ½ pound shrimp · 3 quarts water · 2 strips celery · 5 crabs · ¼ cup chopped ham (optional) · Flour · Salt and pepper to taste · 2 sprigs thyme · 1 bay leaf · 2 cloves

Cut okra into thin rounds and brown in shortening with onion (reserving a small amount), garlic, tomatoes, and tomato paste, stirring constantly. Boil shrimp in 1 quart salted water with the small amount of onion reserved above, and celery. After boiling

about 30 minutes, strain and save stock, and peel shrimp. Boil crabs in 2 quarts salted water. Save stock to combine with shrimp stock. Break crabs in half and add with okra mixture, shrimp, crab, and ham to shrimp-crab stock. Thicken with flour and season with salt and pepper. Add thyme, bay leaf, cloves and simmer gumbo about 2½ hours, stirring often. Serve in a soup bowl with about a teacupful of boiled rice in the center of each bowl.
Serves 10.

GUMBO Z'HERBES

DUNBAR'S

1 bunch collard greens · 1 bunch mustard greens · 1 bunch turnip greens · 1 bunch spinach · 1 bunch water cress · 1 bunch beet tops · 1 bunch carrot tops · 1 bunch parsley · 1 bunch chicory · 1 bunch radish tops · 1 green cabbage · ½ bunch shallots (green onions) · 1 gallon water · 1 pound boiled ham, diced · 1 pound lean veal, diced · 2 tablespoons shortening · 1 large white onion, chopped · 1 tablespoon chopped parsley · 2 bay leaves · 4 sprigs thyme · 2 cloves · 2 allspice · Salt, pepper, and cayenne to taste · Paprika

Wash all greens thoroughly, removing all stems or hard centers of leaves; use only tender parts. Boil greens together in 1 gallon of water about 2 hours. Strain greens and reserve water. Chop greens finely. Simmer ham and veal in shortening about 10 minutes in a deep iron skillet. Add white onion and chopped parsley, cooking

until onion is brown. Add greens and simmer 15 minutes. Add to water from greens the contents of the skillet plus bay leaves, thyme, cloves, allspice, salt, pepper, and cayenne. Bring to a boil and then turn down to a slow boil, cooking over a low flame about 1 hour. Serve in soup bowls, sprinkled with paprika.
Serves 10–12.

OYSTER SOUP

BRENNAN'S

1 cup finely chopped celery · 1 cup finely chopped shallots (green onions) · 1 stick butter · 1 tablespoon flour · 1 teaspoon chopped garlic · Oyster water, plus water to make 6 cups · 2 dozen large oysters · 2 bay leaves · Salt and pepper to taste

Sauté celery and shallots in butter until tender. Blend in flour and cook 5 minutes, stirring over low heat. Add remaining ingredients and simmer 20 minutes. Remove bay leaves and serve.
Makes 1½ quarts.

OYSTER SOUP LAFAYETTE

PONTCHARTRAIN

1 heaping tablespoon butter · 3 shallots (green onions), chopped fine · 1 piece celery, chopped fine · ½ cup minced parsley · 1 heaping tablespoon flour · 2 dozen oysters with liquid · Salt and red pepper · 1 pint water · 2 egg yolks

Sauté in butter the onions, celery, and parsley. Stir in the flour to make a light roux. Cut oysters in thirds, season with salt and red pepper, and add with oyster liquid to roux. Gradually add water and let cook about 3 minutes, or until oysters are cooked through. Remove from fire. Beat the egg yolks lightly and pour the soup into them, whipping all the time. A golden color will result. Lessening the amount of liquid will make a delicious stew.
Makes 4 cups of soup.

RED BEAN SOUP

DUNBAR'S

1 small onion, chopped · ¼ stick butter · ½ pound dried red kidney beans, soaked overnight · 2 cloves garlic, chopped · 2 strips celery, chopped · 2 bay leaves · 2 sprigs thyme · 1 teaspoon Worcestershire sauce · 1 gallon water · ½ pound ham, ground fine · Salt and pepper to taste · 8 tablespoons claret · 2 hard-boiled eggs, sieved · Lemon, sliced thin

Brown onion in butter and add to beans, garlic, celery, bay leaves, thyme, and Worcestershire sauce in 1 gallon water. Simmer about 3 hours, then strain through coarse strainer and mash with large spoon. Add ham and salt and pepper. Put 1 tablespoon of claret in the bottom of each of 8 bouillon cups before pouring soup. Garnish with sieved egg and lemon slice.
Serves 8.

SHRIMP BISQUE

PONTCHARTRAIN

2 pounds shrimp · 1 large onion, chopped · 2 tablespoons chopped celery · 2 tablespoons butter · 2 tablespoons flour · 2 quarts water · ½ cup bread crumbs · Salt and pepper

SHRIMP BALLS: *2 tablespoons chopped shallots (green onions) · ⅛ cup butter · 4 tablespoons fine bread crumbs · 1 egg yolk*

Peel and clean shrimp and run through a meat grinder. Sauté onion and celery in butter, add flour, and cook about 2 minutes. Gradually add water and, when blended, add shrimp. Cook 15–20 minutes. Add bread crumbs, cook a few minutes, remove from fire, and strain to separate liquid and shrimp mixture. Set aside half of shrimp mixture for shrimp balls and put the other half back in soup. Purée, season, and set aside. To make shrimp balls: Sauté shallots in butter and add reserved shrimp mixture and bread crumbs. Moisten with 4 tablespoons soup. Remove from fire and beat in egg yolk. Let cool and roll into balls about the size of walnuts. Heat in oven

at 350° about 5–6 minutes. Put at least 2 shrimp balls in each serving.
Yield: About 2 quarts soup.

COLD SHRIMP AND TOMATO BISQUE

PONTCHARTRAIN

3 tablespoons butter · 4 tablespoons flour · 3½ cups shrimp stock (or water) · 1 pound shrimp · 1 tablespoon tomato paste · 2 teaspoons curry powder · 1 cup light cream · 6 pimento strips · Tomato slices · Halved cooked shrimp

Melt butter in a kettle, stir in flour, and gradually add shrimp stock (water can be substituted if necessary). Bring to a boil, stirring constantly, and then simmer 15 minutes. Peel and devein shrimp and put through a meat grinder. Add to soup, cook about 10 minutes, and then purée. Add tomato paste, curry powder, and cream. Cook a few more minutes, cool and chill. Garnish each serving with pimento strips, tomato slices, and halved shrimp.
Serves 6.

TURTLE SOUP

COMMANDER'S

1 pound turtle meat, cut into 1-inch cubes · 1 cup shortening · 1 cup diced onions · 1 cup diced celery · 6 cloves garlic, chopped · 1 cup flour · 16 ounces tomato sauce · 3 quarts water · ¼ cup B.V. (beef extract) · 2 teaspoons celery salt · 4 bay leaves · 12 cloves · 1 teaspoon thyme · ½ cup chopped parsley · ½ cup Lea & Perrins Sauce · Salt and pepper to taste

GARNISH: *1 cup sherry · 2 lemons quartered and diced thin · 2 chopped hard-boiled eggs*

Sauté turtle in shortening until very brown. Add onions, celery, and garlic and cook 10 minutes. Blend in flour and cook 5 minutes. Add tomato sauce, water, and B.V. and then all other ingredients except sherry, lemon, and eggs. Simmer about 2 hours, or until

meat is very tender. Garnish with lemon and chopped egg and add a little sherry to each serving.
Yield: 1 gallon.

VICHYSSOISE

MASSON'S

1 medium-sized onion, sliced · 2 chopped leeks · 1 piece celery, chopped · 1 bay leaf · Pinch thyme and cayenne · ½ stick butter · 1 raw ham bone · 1 quart milk · 1 pound sliced raw potatoes · 1 egg yolk · Salt · 1 cup heavy cream · Chives or parsley

Sauté onion, leeks, celery, bay leaf, thyme, and cayenne in butter with ham bone. Cook 15–20 minutes. Add boiling milk and potatoes and simmer until potatoes are soft. Pass through fine sieve. Add beaten egg yolk and salt to taste. Chill. Add cream and serve with finely chopped chives or parsley as garnish.
Makes 1½–1¾ quarts.

WATER CRESS SOUP

MASSON'S

Garni of vegetables (1 onion, 1 carrot, and 1 stalk celery tied in cheesecloth) · 1 quart chicken consommé · 1 bunch water cress, cut in half to remove stems · ½ cup white wine · ¼ cup potato flour · Toasted croutons

Simmer garni of vegetables in consommé 15–20 minutes. Remove garni and add water cress and white wine. Simmer 5–10 minutes. Add potato flour and simmer 3–4 minutes. Serve with toasted croutons.
Serves 6.

Eggs

EGGS BOURGUIGNONNE

BRENNAN'S

1/3 cup finely chopped onion · 1/3 cup finely chopped shallots (green onions) · 2 tablespoons minced garlic · 2 tablespoons butter · 1/4 cup flour · 1 cup canned whole tomatoes · 1/4 cup liquid from snails · 1 (4 1/2-ounce) can snails · 1/4 cup diced cooked carrots · Salt and pepper to taste

OMELET: *6 eggs · 3 tablespoons milk or cream · 3/4 teaspoon salt · Dash of pepper · 3 tablespoons butter*

To make Bourguignonne sauce, sauté onion, shallots, and garlic in butter. Blend in flour and brown thoroughly over low heat. Add tomatoes and liquid from snails, then add snails, carrots, salt and pepper and simmer 10–15 minutes, stirring occasionally.
Make three 2-egg omelets and fold 1/4 cup of the Bourguignonne sauce into each omelet. Slide omelets onto serving plates and add more sauce to each.
Serves 3.

EGGS HUSSARDE

BRENNAN'S

2 large thin ham slices, grilled · 2 Holland Rusks · 1/4 cup marchand de vin sauce · 2 slices grilled tomato · 2 soft poached eggs · 1/4 cup Hollandaise sauce · Paprika

Lay a slice of ham across each Holland Rusk and cover with marchand de vin sauce. Lay slices of tomato on the sauce and place poached eggs on tomato slices. Top with Hollandaise sauce and garnish with a sprinkling of paprika.
Serves 1.

EGGS NOUVELLE ORLÉANS

BRENNAN'S

1 stick butter · 1 pound fresh crabmeat · Salt and pepper · 8 eggs · Water · 1 cup vinegar · 1 1/2 cups cream sauce with 1 ounce brandy added

Melt butter in a skillet and add crabmeat and salt and pepper to taste. Sauté the crabmeat about 6 minutes over medium heat. Poach eggs in water and vinegar. Divide sautéed crabmeat among 4 ramekins and cover each portion with 2 poached eggs. Top with brandy cream sauce. Serve immediately with toast or garlic bread.
Serves 4.

EGGS PORTUGUESE

BRENNAN'S

½ bunch shallots (green onions), chopped fine · 1 small white onion, chopped fine · 2 cloves garlic, chopped fine · 1 stick butter · 1 cup peeled tomatoes · ½ cup tomato purée · ¼ bunch celery, chopped fine · 2 teaspoons flour · 2 cups chicken stock · Salt and pepper to taste · 8 patty shells · 8 poached eggs · 2 cups Hollandaise sauce

Sauté shallots and garlic in butter. Add tomatoes, tomato purée, and celery. Blend in flour, then gradually add stock, stirring constantly. Simmer to thicken and season to taste. Warm patty shells just enough to crisp them—if warmed too much, they will crumble. Place sauce in patty shells. Top sauce with poached egg and cover egg with Hollandaise sauce. Serve immediately.
Serves 4.

EGGS ROYAL

BRENNAN'S

1 pound chicken livers, chopped fine · ⅓ cup shallots (green onions), chopped very fine · 3 egg yolks · 8 eggs · 1 cup Demi-Hollandaise sauce

Mix chicken livers, shallots, and egg yolks. Pack into a mold, place mold in a pan of water, and bake at 375° about 25–30 minutes. Unmold and slice like bread. In each of 4 ramekins place 2 slices of the pâté and cover with 2 raw eggs. Bake at 350° about 4 minutes —more or less depending on how soft you like your eggs. After baking top with Demi-Hollandaise sauce, which is made by com-

bining cream sauce with Hollandaise sauce and, after blending, adding 1 ounce of brandy.
Serves 4.

EGGS SARDOU

ANTOINE'S

8 artichoke hearts · 16 anchovy fillets · 8 poached eggs · Hollandaise sauce · ½ cup chopped cooked ham · 1 tablespoon glace de viande or meat glaze · 8 slices truffle

HOLLANDAISE SAUCE: *1 cup clarified butter · 2 tablespoons tarragon vinegar · 1 tablespoon water · 1 tablespoon minced onion · 3 peppercorns · 4 egg yolks · Juice of ¼ lemon*

Put cooked artichoke hearts in a baking pan, place 2 anchovy fillets on each, and warm under low broiler flame. On each artichoke heart, over anchovy fillets, place a poached egg. Cover with Hollandaise sauce, sprinkle with chopped ham and a few drops of glace de viande, and top with a slice of truffle.
Sauce: To clarify butter—slowly melt butter and let stand until clear part can be skimmed off easily. Put vinegar, water, onion, and peppercorns in a saucepan and cook over very low heat to reduce liquid to 1 teaspoon. Remove peppercorns and cool. Add egg yolks, beating slightly. Gradually add butter, beating constantly. Add lemon juice and serve.
Serves either 4 or 8.

EGGS SARDOU*

GALATOIRE'S

6 large artichokes · 1 cup creamed spinach · 6 eggs · Hollandaise sauce

HOLLANDAISE SAUCE: *2 sticks butter · 3 egg yolks · Juice of 1 lemon, strained · Salt, pepper, and cayenne to taste*

* Named for French playwright Victorien Sardou.

Boil artichokes in salted water, drain, and remove chokes and leaves. Fill the hearts with creamed spinach. Poach eggs and place one on each artichoke heart on top of spinach. Cover with Hollandaise sauce, made as follows: In a double boiler gradually add melted butter to egg yolks and lemon juice, stirring constantly until thick. Season to taste and serve over eggs.
Serves 3.

EGGS À LA TURK

BRENNAN'S

1½ sticks butter · ½ cup coarsely chopped chicken livers · ½ cup finely chopped shallots (green onions) · ¾ cup chopped mushrooms · ¼ cup flour · ¾ cup beef stock · ½ teaspoon salt · ½ teaspoon white pepper · ½ cup red wine · 8 eggs · Chopped parsley

Sauté in butter chicken livers, shallots, and mushrooms about 5 minutes. Add flour, stirring constantly over low heat until flour is very brown. Blend in stock, salt, pepper, and wine and simmer 15–20 minutes. Put 2 tablespoons of this sauce in each of 4 shirred-egg dishes. Break 2 eggs in each dish and bake at 350° until eggs are firm. Cover eggs in each dish with 2 more tablespoons of sauce, sprinkle with parsley, and serve.
Serves 4.

OMELETTE ESPAGNOLE

ANTOINE'S

1 (#2) can tomatoes · 3 tablespoons butter · 1 teaspoon salt · Pepper and cayenne · 1 sprig thyme · 1 tablespoon minced parsley · 1 bay leaf · 2 cloves minced garlic · 1 tablespoon flour · 6 chopped shallots or ½ cup minced onion · 5 tablespoons chopped green pepper · ½ cup white wine · ½ cup canned button mushrooms · ½ cup cooked peas · 4 eggs · 1 tablespoon olive oil

Simmer tomatoes and 1 tablespoon butter together 10 minutes, stirring occasionally. Add salt and a few grains of pepper and cayenne and simmer 10 minutes longer. Add thyme, parsley, bay leaf, and garlic and cook 15 minutes, or until sauce is thick.

Melt 1 tablespoon butter, blend in flour, and cook until brown. Add shallots, or onion, and green pepper and brown slightly. Add wine, stirring constantly, and when slightly thickened, add mushrooms and peas. Combine with tomato mixture. Beat eggs until well blended and add tomato mixture. Heat 1 tablespoon butter and olive oil in a skillet and pour in egg-and-tomato mixture. Shake skillet until eggs begin to set, lifting edges of omelette to allow uncooked mixture to flow underneath. When cooked, fold over. Garnish with chopped parsley if desired.

Serves 4.

SEAFOOD OMELET

PONTCHARTRAIN

2 tablespoons chopped shallots (green onions) · 1 tablespoon butter · 4 oysters · 4 large shrimp · 2 ounces lump crabmeat · 4 fresh mushrooms, peeled and sliced · 1 ounce white wine · 1 ounce cream · 3 eggs · 1 tablespoon oil · Salt and pepper to taste

Sauté shallots in butter. Add oysters, shrimp, crabmeat, mushrooms, and wine. Cook until dry, then add cream. Beat eggs until frothy. Preheat oil in an omelet pan, add eggs and seafood. Season, roll omelet, and cook until done.

Serves 2.

Seafood

CRABMEAT IMPERIAL

COMMANDER'S

1 bell (green) pepper, finely diced · 2 pimentos, finely diced · 1 tablespoon English mustard · 1 teaspoon salt · ½ teaspoon white pepper · 2 whole raw eggs · 1 cup mayonnaise · 3 pounds lump crabmeat · Mayonnaise · Paprika

Mix together well bell pepper, pimentos, mustard, salt, white pepper, eggs, and mayonnaise. Add crabmeat and mix well with fingers so that the lumps are not broken. Divide mixture into 8 crab shells or ramekins, heaping it in lightly. Coat the tops with a little mayonnaise and sprinkle with paprika. Bake 15 minutes at 350°. Serve hot or cold.
Serves 8.

CRABMEAT MONACO

ARNAUD'S

1 chopped shallot (green onion) · 3 sliced mushrooms · 2 tablespoons olive oil · 3 tablespoons canned tomatoes · 4 ounces crabmeat · Salt and white pepper · 1 tablespoon sherry · 1 slice toast

Sauté shallot and mushrooms in oil, add tomatoes, and cook about 5 minutes. Add crabmeat and cook 5 minutes longer. Season to taste and stir in sherry. Serve in a casserole dish with toast triangles on either side.
Serves 1.

STUFFED CRAB

BRENNAN'S

1 medium-sized onion, chopped fine · ½ cup shallots (green onions), chopped fine · 1 stick butter · 2 cups coarse bread crumbs, dampened with oyster water or fish stock · 2 bay leaves · ½ teaspoon salt · ½ teaspoon black pepper · Dash cayenne · ½ pound crabmeat · 1 tablespoon chopped parsley · ½ cup buttered bread crumbs

In a medium-sized skillet sauté onion and shallots in butter. Add dampened bread crumbs and cook 3–5 minutes. Add bay leaves, salt, pepper, cayenne, crabmeat, and parsley, mix thoroughly, and heat through. Remove from heat and remove bay leaves. Pack stuffing into 4 crab shells and cover with buttered bread crumbs. Bake in a shallow baking dish 15–20 minutes at 350°.
Serves 4.

FROGS' LEGS BELLE MEUNIÈRE

MASSON'S

8 pairs medium frogs' legs · Salt and pepper · 1 stick butter · ¼ cup chopped shallots (green onions) · ¼ cup sliced mushrooms · ¼ cup white wine · Juice of 1 lemon · 3 teaspoons cognac · 1 tablespoon chopped parsley

Separate frogs' legs and season with salt and pepper. Sauté slowly in butter until brown. Add shallots and mushrooms and simmer 5 minutes. Add wine and lemon and again simmer 5 minutes. Stir in cognac and sprinkle with chopped parsley.
Serves 4.

FROGS' LEGS RICHELIEU

COMMANDER'S

8 pairs frogs' legs · ¼ cup flour · 1 stick butter · 2 cloves garlic, chopped · 4 chopped shallots (green onions) · ¼ pound mushrooms · ½ pound chicken livers · ½ stick butter · 1 pint brown sauce · 1 tablespoon chopped parsley · ½ cup claret · Salt and pepper

Dredge frogs' legs in flour and sauté in butter until golden brown. Add garlic and cook until half browned. Add shallots and mushrooms and cook 3 minutes. Sauté chicken livers and add to frogs' legs. Add brown sauce, parsley and wine and simmer until done. Season to taste.
Serves 4.

LOBSTER DIAVOLO

MASSON'S

2 (2–2½-pound) lobsters, · Fish stock or water · 1 stick butter · ¼ cup white wine · ½ cup chopped shallots (green onions) · 1 clove chopped garlic · ½ cup sliced mushrooms · 1 bay leaf · Pinch each oregano and basil · 4 tablespoons olive oil · 2 cups canned Italian tomatoes, peeled and cored · Salt and pepper

Boil lobsters in fish stock or water. Cut in half lengthwise and remove meat from bodies and claws. Simmer meat in ½ stick butter and white wine. In another pan, sauté green onions, garlic, mushrooms, bay leaf, oregano, and basil in the remaining butter and olive oil. Cook until shallots are soft, add tomatoes, and season to taste. Combine meat with sauce and simmer 6–8 minutes. Serve in cleaned shells or in a casserole.
Serves 4.

ARTICHOKE AND OYSTER CASSEROLE

PONTCHARTRAIN

2 sticks butter · 1 cup flour · 1 quart milk · ½ pint breakfast (light) cream · 6 dozen oysters, drained · 2 teaspoons salt · 1 teaspoon black pepper · 1 dash Tabasco sauce · 2 teaspoons Worcestershire sauce · ½ cup sherry · 8 fresh cooked artichoke hearts, finely chopped · Artichoke leaves · Bread crumbs

Melt butter and blend in flour. Remove from fire and slowly add milk and cream (which have been combined and heated). Heat oysters to remove excess liquid and add to cream sauce. Simmer about 5 minutes and add seasoning, sherry, and artichoke hearts. Pour into a casserole dish, arrange artichoke leaves all around the edge of dish, sprinkle with bread crumbs, and bake 10 minutes at 350°.
Serves 8.

GRATIN OF OYSTERS AND MUSHROOMS

PONTCHARTRAIN

1 shredded bell (green) pepper · 3 chopped shallots (green onions) · 4 tablespoons butter · ½ pound small whole mushrooms · 1 quart oysters · Salt and pepper

4 tablespoons butter · 4 tablespoons flour · 1½ cups heavy cream · 1 cup breakfast (light) cream · 2 tablespoons grated Parmesan cheese · Pinch nutmeg · Pinch paprika · 1 teaspoon Pernod · Bread crumbs

Sauté bell pepper and shallots in butter. After 2–3 minutes add mushrooms and oysters, season to taste, and cook slowly about 4 minutes. In the top of a double boiler, melt butter and blend in flour, stirring constantly. Slowly add cream, grated cheese, nutmeg, and paprika. Cook, stirring, until thickened. Add sautéed bell pepper, onions, mushrooms, and oysters, then add Pernod. Pour into a baking dish and sprinkle with bread crumbs. Brown under broiler and serve.
Serves 8.

OYSTER PAN ROAST

MANALE'S

6–8 shallots (green onions), chopped · 1 bunch parsley, chopped · ½ pound margarine · 3 cups flour · 4 cups water (approximately) · Salt and pepper · 6 dozen oysters · Bread crumbs

Sauté shallots and parsley in margarine, stir in flour, and blend in water to make a thick sauce. Season to taste. Boil oysters until edges curl and drain. Put 6 oysters in each of 12 individual casserole dishes or ramekins and cover each portion with sauce. Sprinkle with bread crumbs and bake about 20 minutes at 350°.
Serves 12.

To make Manale's Combination Pan Roast, add 1 pound crabmeat to sauce.

OYSTERS POULETTE

COMMANDER'S

2½ dozen oysters with liquid · ½ stick butter · 1 cup hot milk · 3 tablespoons flour · Juice of ½ lemon · 1 egg yolk · Salt to taste · 4 patty shells or 4 slices toast

Heat oysters until edges curl and then drain. Make a cream sauce with butter, milk, and flour. Blend in lemon juice, egg yolk, and salt. Add oysters to heat thoroughly, but do not boil. Serve in patty shells or on toast.
Serves 4.

COURTBOUILLON LOUISIANA

ANTOINE'S

1 tablespoon butter · 1 tablespoon flour · 2 large onions, chopped · 1 clove garlic, minced · 1 teaspoon thyme · 1 teaspoon parsley · 1 teaspoon allspice · 2 bay leaves · 1 quart water · 1 cup dry red wine · 6 large fresh tomatoes, finely chopped · 6 slices red fish or red snapper (about 3 pounds) · Juice of 1 lemon · Salt and cayenne to taste

Make a roux by melting butter in a heavy pot, adding the flour and cooking very slowly until it attains a brownish hue. Add onions, garlic, and seasoning and cook a few minutes. Then add the water, wine, and tomatoes. Let simmer 1 hour and then add slices of raw fish. Add lemon juice and seasoning, simmer 15 minutes, and serve in soup bowls with French bread.
Serves 6.

RED FISH COURTBOUILLON

BRENNAN'S

½ cup vegetable oil · 1 cup chopped celery · 2 cups chopped bell (green) pepper · 1¾ cups chopped white onion · 1 cup finely chopped shallots (green onions) · 2 tablespoons minced garlic ·

4 bay leaves · ¾ teaspoon powdered thyme · 3 cups canned whole tomatoes · ¼ teaspoon black pepper · 2 teaspoons salt · ½ teaspoon cayenne · 2 tablespoons paprika · 4 cups fish stock · 4 pounds red fish (clean and fillet fish, using bones, skin, and head for making stock) · Seasoned flour · 3 tablespoons lemon juice · ¾ cup Burgundy · 1 lemon, sliced

In a large pot or a large deep skillet heat oil and sauté celery, bell pepper, onion, shallots, and garlic. Stir in bay leaves, thyme, tomatoes, pepper, salt, cayenne, and paprika and simmer 5 minutes. Stir in stock and cook slowly 25–30 minutes. While cooking sauce, lightly coat red fish with seasoned flour and sear on both sides on hot grill, lower heat, and continue cooking until almost done; remove and keep warm. When sauce has cooked approximately 30 minutes, stir in lemon juice and Burgundy. Add fish and cook slowly 10–12 minutes more. Garnish with lemon slices and serve with hot fluffy rice.
Serves 4 or 5.

COLD RED FISH BAYOU

BRENNAN'S

1 (4-pound) red fish · 2 bay leaves · Sprig of thyme · Piece of celery · 1 medium-sized onion, halved · 1 lemon, cut in half · 1 can chopped pimentos · 1 bunch shallots (green onions), chopped · 2 tablespoons chopped parsley · Salt and pepper · 2 tablespoons unflavored gelatin · Sliced tomatoes · Hard-boiled eggs · Remoulade sauce

Put red fish in a pot and cover with cold water. Add bay leaves, thyme, celery, and onion. Squeeze lemon, then drop in the halves,

rind and all. Boil 20 minutes, remove from fire, and allow to cool. Remove fish from stock and pick all meat off bones. To the picked fish, add pimentos, shallots, parsley, and salt and pepper to taste. Mix well. Soften gelatin in cold water and add to fish stock. Reboil, then strain through a cloth. Pour into a mold to cover fish mixture and chill 2–3 hours. Unmold on a platter and garnish with sliced tomatoes and hard-boiled eggs, and top with remoulade sauce.
Serves 6.

RED FISH À LA GREIG

COMMANDER'S

1 (8-pound) red fish, boned and filleted · 2 sticks butter · Juice of 2 lemons · 1 pound lump crabmeat · 3 teaspoons chopped parsley · Salt to taste

Cut red fish into 6 portions, sprinkle with salt, brush with 1 stick melted butter, and broil 10 minutes or until brown. Melt remaining butter, add lemon juice and crabmeat, and heat thoroughly. Pour over fish, sprinkle with parsley, and serve hot.
Serves 6.

FILLET OF RED FISH WITH HOLLANDAISE SAUCE

ARNAUD'S

3 pounds fillet red snapper · Water to cover · Salt and white pepper ·

6 egg yolks · 1 teaspoon dry mustard · 1¼ ounces tarragon vinegar · 4 sticks butter · Paprika

Poach fish in water until it flakes easily. Season to taste, drain, and place on platter, keeping warm.
Combine egg yolks, mustard, and vinegar and beat well. Continue beating and gradually add butter. Cook, stirring over low heat until sauce thickens. Pour over fish and sprinkle with paprika.
Serves 4.

BAKED RED FISH WITH TOMATO SAUCE

PONTCHARTRAIN

1 (4–5 pound) red fish · Salt and pepper · 1 tablespoon butter · 1 tablespoon lard

SAUCE: *3 slices bacon · 2 large white onions, chopped very fine · 2 cans tomatoes · 1 sprig chopped parsley · 1 sprig chopped thyme · 2 bay leaves · Salt and pepper · Hard-boiled egg · Lemon slices*

Clean fish well inside and out. Split on underside so that seasoning can penetrate well, and rub inside and out with salt and pepper. Put in a baking pan, spread with butter and lard, and bake about 15 minutes at 400° before covering with sauce.

To make sauce: Fry bacon in skillet. Remove bacon and fry onions in bacon fat. When onions are browned, add tomatoes. Cook a few minutes and add parsley, thyme, bay leaves, chopped bacon, and salt and pepper. Let cook until all water has cooked out of tomatoes. Add this sauce to fish in oven, now lowered to 350°. Baste fish with sauce while baking, about 45 minutes, adding a little water from time to time if necessary. Garnish with slices of hard-boiled egg and lemon. May be served on toast if desired.

Serves 6.

RED SNAPPER CHAMBORD

ARNAUD'S

1 (4-pound) red snapper · 3 shallots (green onions), minced · 1 clove garlic, minced · 3 sprigs parsley, chopped fine · 12 ounces lump crabmeat · 12 ounces shrimp · 3 slices soaked bread · 4 tablespoons butter · Salt and pepper · Lemon slices · Parsley sprigs

SAUCE: *2 shallots (green onions), chopped fine · 10 fresh mushrooms, chopped · ½ pound shrimp, chopped · 2 tablespoons butter · ½ pint white wine · Salt and pepper*

Split fish and remove bone. Sauté about 30 minutes the shallots, garlic, parsley, crabmeat, shrimp, and bread squeezed out in water. Stuff into red snapper, season, and bake 1 hour, basting often. Place on a platter, garnish with lemon and parsley.

Sauté shallots, mushrooms, and shrimp in butter, add wine, stir well, and season to taste. Pour some of this sauce over fish and serve the remainder in a gravy boat.
Serves 6.

RED SNAPPER PONTCHARTRAIN

PONTCHARTRAIN

1 (8-ounce) fillet of red snapper · 1 medium-sized soft-shell crab · Milk · Flour · Salt and white pepper · Shortening

SAUCE MEUNIÈRE: *½ stick butter · Juice of ½ lemon · 1 teaspoon chopped parsley · Dash Worcestershire sauce*

Dip red snapper and soft-shell crab in milk, then in flour, and sprinkle with salt and pepper. Melt shortening in a saucepan, and when well heated sauté red snapper and crab until golden brown on both sides.
To make sauce: Melt butter in a saucepan and cook until golden brown. Add all other ingredients, pour over red snapper and crab, and serve.
Serves 1.
Red Snapper Pontchartrain is a variation of Pompano Pontchartrain, which is made by the same recipe with pompano instead of red snapper and a buster instead of a soft-shell crab. ("Buster" is the name given to a crab when it is in the stage between hard shell and soft shell.)

SHRIMP À LA CREOLE

DUNBAR'S

3 pounds shrimp · 1 tablespoon shortening · 1 medium-sized onion, chopped · 2 strips celery, chopped · 1 pod garlic, minced · 1 small bell (green) pepper, chopped · ½ can tomatoes · ½ can tomato paste · 3 sprigs thyme · 1 bay leaf · 1 tablespoon chopped parsley · ½ tablespoon sugar · Salt and pepper to taste · Boiled rice

Boil shrimp approximately 10 minutes, peel, and clean. Melt shortening in a skillet and add onion, celery, garlic, and bell pepper. Simmer 5 minutes and add tomatoes, tomato paste, thyme, bay leaf, parsley, sugar, and salt and pepper. Mix well and add shrimp. Simmer ½ hour and serve in a circle of boiled rice.
Serves 6.

SHRIMP À L'IMPÉRATRICE

COMMANDER'S

1 pound boiled shrimp, peeled and deveined · 1 (5-ounce) bell (green) pepper, chopped · 3 pimentos, chopped · 1 tablespoon dry mustard · 1 teaspoon salt · 1 pint mayonnaise · 1 quart Duchess potatoes (mashed potatoes mixed with an egg yolk) · 6 peeled avocado halves · Bread crumbs mixed with paprika

Mix shrimp, bell pepper, pimentos, mustard, and salt into mayonnaise. Lay a border of Duchess potatoes around each of 6 ramekins and place a half avocado in the center of each. Fill avocado with shrimp mixture and sprinkle with paprika crumbs. Bake in a moderate oven 10 minutes. Can be used as a cold dish without the potatoes.
Serves 6.

SHRIMP À L'ORLÉANS

COMMANDER'S

½ pound cooked lobster meat · 1½ pounds peeled boiled shrimp · 4 ounces sliced mushrooms · 1½ sticks butter · ½ bunch shallots (green onions), chopped · 1 cup flour · 1 pint hot milk · 2 cups oyster liquid · 1 cup sherry · ¼ cup lemon juice · 2 egg yolks · 2 tablespoons chopped parsley · Salt and cayenne pepper · 6 patty shells

Sauté lobster, shrimp, and mushrooms in ½ stick melted butter. Put aside. Sauté shallots in 1 stick melted butter and blend in flour. Cook 2 minutes, being careful not to brown. Stirring constantly,

gradually add hot milk, oyster liquid, sherry, and lemon juice. Add lobster, shrimp, and mushrooms and simmer 10 minutes. Add beaten egg yolks, parsley, and salt and pepper to taste. Remove tops from patty shells and fill with seafood and sauce.
Serves 6.

STUFFED SHRIMP

MANALE'S

2 onions, chopped · 2 bell (green) peppers, chopped · 4 or 5 pieces celery, chopped · 4 pods garlic, chopped · 1 cup chopped parsley · ½ pound margarine · 1 pound raw shrimp, chopped · ½ loaf stale French bread, squeezed out in water · 2 eggs · 1 pound crabmeat · Salt and pepper · 3 dozen raw shrimp · Flour · Egg-milk wash · Deep fat

Sauté onions, bell peppers, celery, garlic, and parsley in margarine. Add shrimp and cook 10 minutes. Add wet bread, then eggs, and cook 5 minutes, stirring constantly. Add crabmeat and season to taste. Peel shrimp to tail only, split halfway through, and open up (or fantail). Pile each shrimp with a mound of stuffing and freeze until hard.
Dip frozen stuffed shrimp in flour, then in egg-milk wash, then in flour again. Fry in deep fat until golden brown.
Serves 12.
Stuffed Flounder: Same stuffing; 12 flounders—split, stuff, broil.

SHRIMP VICTORIA

BRENNAN'S

½ bunch shallots (green onions), chopped · 2 tablespoons butter · ½ cup white wine · 1 cup cream sauce · ½ cup cooked mushrooms, sliced in half · 16 medium-sized boiled shrimp · ½ cup sour cream · 1 tablespoon chopped parsley · Pinch of thyme

Sauté shallots in butter. Add wine and blend in cream sauce. Add mushrooms and shrimp and blend in sour cream. Add parsley and thyme and serve with parsley rice in individual copper casseroles.
Serves 2.

TROUT ALEXANDER

COMMANDER'S

1 (3-pound) speckled trout, cleaned, skinned, and boned · Milk · Water · Salt · 3 bay leaves · ¾ pound sliced mushrooms · 1 stick butter · 1 clove garlic, minced · 4 whole shallots (green onions), chopped · ¼ pound cooked shrimp · ¼ pound cooked lobster · 2 tablespoons flour · 1 cup milk · 1 cup cream · Salt and pepper to taste · 2 ounces sherry · 4 sprigs parsley, chopped

Lay pieces of trout side by side in a shallow buttered saucepan. Add enough milk to half cover fish, and about half as much water as milk. Sprinkle lightly with salt, add bay leaves, and cover pan. Bring liquid to a boil, reduce heat, and simmer slowly about 15 minutes, or until fish flakes readily. Remove fish and set aside to keep warm. Reduce broth to ½ cup and reserve for use in sauce.

Sauté mushrooms in butter 5 minutes. Add garlic and shallots and simmer 5 minutes until tender. Add shrimp and lobster and heat thoroughly. Sprinkle flour over all and cook, stirring, 2 minutes. Gradually add milk, cream, and reduced fish broth and bring to a boil, stirring constantly. Reduce heat and simmer about 10 minutes, stirring occasionally. Season to taste, add sherry and parsley, pour over fish on a platter, and serve at once.

Serves 4.

TROUT AMANDINE

COMMANDER'S

1 (3-pound) fillet of trout · 1 stick butter · 4 tablespoons sliced almonds · Juice of ½ lemon · 1 teaspoon chopped parsley

Sauté trout in ½ stick butter until golden brown and cooked through. Put aside and keep hot. Brown almonds in remaining ½ stick butter and add lemon juice. Pour over trout, sprinkle with parsley, and serve at once.

Serves 2.

TROUT MEUNIÈRE AMANDINE

GALATOIRE'S

3 (2½-pound) trout · Milk · Flour · Salt and pepper · 2 sticks butter · Juice of 2 lemons · 1 tablespoon chopped parsley · 6 ounces shelled almonds

Skin and fillet trout, dip in cold milk, sprinkle with flour, and season with salt and pepper. Melt butter in a skillet and fry fillets of trout slowly until brown on both sides. Remove fish to a warm platter. To the butter remaining in the pan, add lemon juice and parsley. Slice almonds, roast until brown, sprinkle over fish, pour over brown butter, and serve.
Serves 6.

TROUT BLANGÉ

BRENNAN'S

1 stick butter · 1 tablespoon minced garlic · ¾ cup peeled raw shrimp · ¾ cup raw oysters · ½ cup sliced mushrooms · ½ teaspoon Spanish saffron · 2 cups canned whole tomatoes · 1 cup fish stock · ¼ teaspoon cayenne · 1 teaspoon salt · 2 tablespoons cornstarch · ¼ cup water · 1 tablespoon chopped parsley · 2 (2-pound) trout · 2 cups seasoned mashed potatoes · 8 whole cooked mushrooms · 8 whole cooked shrimp

Sauté in butter in a large skillet garlic, shrimp, oysters, mushrooms, and saffron. Add tomatoes, fish stock, cayenne, and salt. Simmer 15–20 minutes. Combine cornstarch and water and add to thicken sauce. Remove from heat, add parsley, and keep warm. Broil trout to a golden brown and place on a warm serving platter. Flute a wall of mashed potatoes around rim of platter. Cover fish with sauce and garnish with whole mushrooms and shrimp. Sprinkle potatoes with paprika and brown under broiler.
Serves 4.

FILLET OF TROUT

DUNBAR'S

1 (6-ounce) trout fillet per person · 2 tablespoons shortening · Water to cover trout

SAUCE: *4 sticks butter · 3 hard-boiled eggs, sieved · 1 can anchovy fillets, mashed · 1 bottle capers · Juice of 2 lemons · 1 tablespoon horseradish mustard · 1 tablespoon Worcestershire sauce · 1 pod garlic, minced · 1 tablespoon onion juice*
GARNISH: *Parsley · Pimentos · Lemon quarters*

Wash fillets well and bake, submerged in water and shortening, at 350° about 10 minutes, or until done.
Melt butter in a saucepan and add all remaining sauce ingredients. Simmer very slowly about 15 minutes. Remove trout from water and shortening, drain, and place on a heated plate. Pour sauce over trout and garnish with parsley, pimento strips, and lemon quarters.
Sauce serves 15.

TROUT EUGÈNE

PONTCHARTRAIN

1 (7–8 pound) trout fillet · 1 stick butter · 1 shallot (green onion), cut fine · 4 large peeled shrimp · Juice of ½ lemon · 1 teaspoon chopped parsley · 2 ounces lump crabmeat

Sauté trout in ½ stick butter. Put aside and keep warm. Melt remaining butter and add shallot, shrimp, and lemon juice. Cook about 5–6 minutes. Add parsley and crabmeat and toss with shrimp. Cover trout with mixture and serve.
Serves 1.

TROUT MARGUERY

GALATOIRE'S

1 (2½-pound) trout · 1 tablespoon olive oil · 1 cup water · 2 sticks butter · 3 egg yolks · Juice of 1 lemon, strained · Salt, pepper, and cayenne · 12 shrimp · 2 truffles · ½ can mushrooms

Skin and fillet trout and place the folded fillets in a pan with olive oil and water. Bake in a hot oven about 15 minutes. To make Hollandaise sauce: Put beaten egg yolks and lemon juice in a double boiler over hot water and gradually add melted butter, stirring constantly until thickened. Add seasoning, shrimp, truffles, and mushrooms, cut into small pieces, to sauce and pour over fish and serve. Serves 2.

SUPREME OF TROUT, CRABMEAT SAUCE

MASSON'S

4 (6–8-ounce) trout fillets · Salt and pepper · 2 lemons · ½ cup chopped shallots (green onions) · 1 stick butter · ½ cup white wine · 2 cups heavy cream · Salt and pepper · 2 or 3 egg yolks · ½ pound crabmeat

Sprinkle trout fillets with salt and pepper, squeeze ½ lemon over each, and broil until done. Sauté onions in butter until soft. Gradually stir in wine and cream and simmer 5–8 minutes. Season to taste. Remove from fire and stir in beaten egg yolks. Fold in crabmeat and spoon over broiled fillets.
Serves 4.

FILLET DE TRUIT VENDÔME

ARNAUD'S

1 (2-pound) trout, skinned and boned · Juice of ½ lemon · ½ pound crabmeat · ½ pound chopped boiled shrimp · 4 teaspoons chopped chives · 4 ounces fresh mushrooms · 1 stick butter · Salt and pepper · 1½ ounces red wine

Cut trout into 4 pieces and cook in water with lemon juice 15–20 minutes. Place on platter and keep warm. Sauté crabmeat, shrimp, chives, and mushrooms in butter, season to taste, and cook 15 minutes. Add wine and simmer 5 minutes. Pour sauce over fish and serve.
Serves 4.

TROUT VÉRONIQUE

PONTCHARTRAIN

1 trout fillet (from a 1½-pound trout) · ½ pint white wine · ½ cup rich Hollandaise sauce · 8 seedless grapes

Poach trout in wine in a pan small enough so that wine covers trout. After poaching about 7 minutes, remove trout, draining well, and place on an ovenproof serving plate. Reduce remaining liquid over a fast fire to 2 cooking spoons of liquid. Add Hollandaise sauce and stir briskly. Place grapes on trout, cover with sauce, and glaze quickly in broiler.
Serves 1.

BOUILLABAISE

COMMANDER'S

*3 pounds fillet of red fish · 4 soft-shell crabs · ½ pound shrimp · ½ pound scallops · 1 small lobster tail · ¾ cup olive oil · 3 tablespoons flour · 1 cup chopped onions · 1 cup chopped celery · 3 cloves garlic · 3 cups crushed tomatoes · 2 pints water · 1 cup dry white wine · 3 bay leaves · 3 tablespoons finely chopped parsley · ½ teaspoon saffron · ¼ teaspoon cayenne pepper · 2 teaspoons salt · 8 rounds Parmesan cheese toast**

Sauté all seafood in ½ cup olive oil until half done, stir in flour, remove from heat and put aside. Sauté onions, celery, and garlic in re-

* Cut French bread into ¼-inch slices, butter, sprinkle with cheese, and brown under broiler.

maining olive oil. Add tomatoes and cook 5 minutes. Add water and other ingredients and simmer a few minutes before adding all seafood. Cook 10 minutes longer and serve with cheese toast on top. Serves 8.

BOUILLABAISE DE POMPANO MADELON

ARNAUD'S

2 shallots (green onions), chopped fine · 4 tablespoons olive oil · ½ cup tomatoes · 8 chopped raw shrimp · 8 chopped raw oysters · 1 boiled lobster, chopped large · ½ tablespoon saffron · 2 cups fish stock · 1 (2-pound) pompano, split · 2 busters · Salt and pepper · 2 slices toast · Chopped parsley*

Sauté shallots in oil, add tomatoes, cook a few minutes, and add shrimp, oysters, lobster, and saffron. Cook 10 minutes and add fish stock. Broil pompano and busters about 5 minutes, add to sauce, and cook 5 minutes longer. Season to taste and serve on deep oval platters with toast triangles and chopped parsley garnish.
Serves 2.

BUSTERS BÉARNAISE

BRENNAN'S

9 busters, cleaned and dried · 1 egg · 1 cup milk · Flour · 1 stick butter · 6 buttered toast triangles · 1½ cups Béarnaise sauce · 1 tablespoon chopped parsley*

Dip busters in batter of beaten egg and milk. Dredge in flour and fry in butter until golden brown. Mount on toast triangles and cover with Béarnaise sauce. Sprinkle with parsley.
Serves 3.

* "Buster" is the name given to the crab when it is in the stage between hard and soft shell.

CRAWFISH ÉTOUFÉE

BRENNAN'S

2 sticks butter · 1 cup finely chopped white onion · ½ cup finely chopped celery · 1 cup finely chopped shallots (green onions) · 1 teaspoon minced garlic · 2 tablespoons flour · 1 cup whole tomatoes · 2 cups fish stock · 2 teaspoons salt · 1 teaspoon black pepper · Dash cayenne · 1 tablespoon Worcestershire sauce · 1½ cups crawfish meat

In a large saucepan sauté in butter the onion, celery, and shallots until tender. Add garlic and cook 1 minute more. Stir in flour, stirring constantly until golden brown. Add tomatoes and brown. Blend in stock and simmer 10 minutes. Add salt, pepper, cayenne, Worcestershire sauce, and crawfish. Cook slowly 15–20 minutes, stirring occasionally. Serve with hot fluffy rice.
Serves 3 or 4.

STUFFED FLOUNDER

COMMANDER'S

1 cup minced onions · ½ cup minced shallots (green onions) · 1½ cups minced celery · 3 cloves minced garlic · ⅕ bunch chopped parsley · ½ pound margarine · 2 tablespoons flour · 1 cup milk · 1 cup dry white wine · ½ cup chopped boiled shrimp · ½ cup lump crabmeat · 2½ cups bread crumbs · Salt and pepper to taste · 6 (1-pound) flounders · 18 peeled boiled shrimp

Sauté onion, shallots, celery, garlic, and parsley in margarine. Add flour and blend in well. Gradually stir in milk and wine, cooking until thickened. Add shrimp and crabmeat and thicken further with bread crumbs. Season to taste.
Split each flounder and fill with dressing. Top each fish with 3 whole shrimp and cook under broiler about 20 minutes, or until fish is cooked through.
Serves 6.

POISSON EN CHEMISE

BRENNAN'S

2 fish fillets · 1–1½ cups white wine · 1 egg yolk · 2 tablespoons grated Parmesan cheese · 1 cup thick cream sauce · ½ cup chopped cooked carrots · ½ cup chopped cooked mushrooms · Salt and pepper to taste · 2 large crêpes · ½ cup velouté de poisson (cream sauce made with fish stock). ½ cup Hollandaise sauce · 1 tablespoon parsley · Salt and pepper

Poach fish in white wine. Put fish aside to keep warm and reserve stock to make velouté sauce. Blend egg yolk and grated cheese with cream sauce and add carrots, mushrooms, salt and pepper to make chemise dressing. Place poached fish in pan and cover each piece with chemise dressing and then a crêpe. Blend velouté de poisson with Hollandaise sauce and parsley. Season, pour over fish and crêpes, and bake until heated through.
Serves 2.

POMPANO GRAND DUC

BRENNAN'S

¼ cup finely chopped shallots (green onions) · 3 tablespoons butter · ¼ cup flour · ¾ cup fish stock · 3 tablespoons white wine · ¼ teaspoon salt · Dash cayenne · 1 egg yolk · 2 cups seasoned mashed potatoes · 6 warm green asparagus spears · 1 (1½-pound) poached fillet of pompano · 6 boiled shrimp · 6 scalded oysters · ½ cup Hollandaise sauce · ½ cup unsweetened whipped cream

Sauté shallots in butter. Blend in flour and cook slowly about 5 minutes, stirring constantly to prevent browning. Remove from heat and blend in fish stock, wine, salt, and cayenne. When smooth, blend in beaten egg yolk. Return to low heat and cook about 15 minutes, stirring constantly.
Flute a wall of mashed potatoes around edge of large warm platter. Place bundle of asparagus in center and cover with fish sauce. Place pompano on top of sauce and garnish with shrimp and oysters.

Combine Hollandaise sauce and whipped cream and pour over fish. Bake at 375° until potatoes are lightly browned.
Serves 3 or 4.

POMPANO EN PAPILLOTE

ANTOINE'S

3 medium-sized pompanos · 3 cups water · 1 chopped shallot or 2 tablespoons chopped onion · 6 tablespoons butter · 2¼ cups white wine · 1 cup crabmeat · 1 cup diced cooked shrimp · ½ clove garlic, minced · 1½ cups chopped onions · Pinch thyme · 1 bay leaf · 2 cups fish stock · 2 tablespoons flour · 2 egg yolks · Salt and pepper*

Clean pompanos and cut into 6 fillets, removing head and backbone. Simmer heads and bones in water until there are 2 cups stock. Sauté fillets with shallot in 2 tablespoons butter and add 2 cups wine. Cover and simmer slowly until fillets are tender, about 5–8 minutes. Sauté crabmeat, shrimp, and ¼ clove garlic in 2 tablespoons butter. Add onion and remaining garlic and cook 10 minutes. Add thyme, bay leaf, and 1¾ cups fish stock, and simmer 10 minutes. Melt 2 tablespoons butter, blend in flour, and gradually stir in remaining ¼ cup fish stock. Add to crabmeat mixture with wine stock drained from fillets. Simmer, stirring constantly until thickened. Beat egg yolks and mix with sauce and remaining ¼ cup wine. Add salt and pepper to taste. Chill in refrigerator until firm. Cut 6 parchment-paper hearts 12 inches long and 8 inches wide. Oil paper well. Place sauce (divided into 6 portions) on one side of heart, lay fillet on sauce, and fold over other half of paper. Seal edges of paper by folding over and pinching together all around. Lay sealed hearts on an oiled baking sheet and bake at 450° 15 minutes, or until paper hearts are browned. Serve at once, cutting open paper at table.
Serves 6.

* Fresh salmon, sea trout, or striped bass may be used when pompano is unavailable.

LA BELLE SOLE DE LA MANCHE À LA NEPTUNE*

ANTOINE'S

*6 raw fillets of sole · 1 cup fish stock** · ½ cup dry white wine · Juice of ½ lemon · 1 cup heavy cream · Salt and pepper to taste · 12 cucumber sticks, parboiled and cooked in butter*

Season sole fillets with salt and pepper, fold in half, and place in a large buttered saucepan. Pour fish stock and wine over fillets. Cook slowly 5–6 minutes, until fish is done. Transfer fish to a serving platter and keep warm. Add lemon to the liquid in which the fish was poached, continue cooking until it is reduced to about ½ cup. Add the cream, cook a while longer, and season to taste. Arrange the cooked cucumber sticks on either side of the fish, pour sauce over all, and serve immediately.
Serves 6.

* Created for a dinner of the Chevaliers du Tastevin.
** Made with bones, heads, and trimmings of sole.

LES MERVEILLES DE LA MER EN CRÊPES

MASSON'S

½ cup chopped shallots (green onions) · ½ cup sliced mushrooms · 3 sticks butter · 3 tablespoons flour · ½ cup white wine · 1 quart light cream · 3 or 4 egg yolks · Salt and pepper · ½ pound cooked lobster meat · ½ pound cooked shrimp (pieces) · ½ pound crabmeat · 2 teaspoons cognac · 8 crêpes

Sauté shallots and mushrooms in 2 sticks butter. Add flour and cook 2–3 minutes. Gradually add wine and cream and simmer 8–10 minutes. Remove from fire and stir in beaten egg yolks, adding enough to make a sauce of medium consistency. Season to taste. Sauté seafood in 1 stick butter 4–5 minutes. Add cognac and ignite. After cognac burns out, add half of the sauce to the seafood mixture. Divide this onto crêpes and roll up. Cover crêpes with the remainder of the sauce.
Serves 4.

SOFT-SHELL TURTLE STEW

COMMANDER'S

6 pounds soft-shell turtle · ½ cup oil or shortening · 1 medium-sized garlic cluster, chopped · 1 stalk celery, chopped · 1 pound onions, chopped · 1½ cups flour · 1½ cups tomato purée · Water to cover · Salt and pepper · 1 small spice bag (thyme, bay leaf, cloves, and allspice in cheesecloth) · 1 cup brandy · ¼ cup sherry · ¼ cup white wine · 16 whole cooked mushrooms · 16 slices crisp bacon · 8 teaspoons chopped parsley

Braise turtle in oil until brown in oven at 400°. Add garlic, celery, and onions and cook about 15 minutes at 350°. Stir in flour and cook 4–5 minutes. Add tomato purée, seasoning and spices, and water to cover. Cook until turtle is tender, season to taste, add wine, and simmer 3–4 minutes. Cut the soft shell of turtle into strips, boil until tender, and add to the stew. Garnish with mushrooms, bacon strips, and parsley and serve with toast or rice.
Serves 8.

Fowl

POULET À L'ARMAGNAC

BRENNAN'S

¼ cup chopped shallots (green onions) · ½ cup sliced fresh mushrooms · 2 pats butter · 1 roast chicken (split, main bones removed) · 1 jigger Armagnac · 1 cup chicken velouté (cream sauce made with chicken stock) · Salt and pepper

Sauté shallots and mushrooms in butter. Place the halves of roast chicken in the pan and flame with Armagnac. Stir in velouté, season to taste, and simmer 1–2 minutes.
Serves 2.

CHICKEN BOSTONIAN

ARNAUD'S

½ chicken · 3 tablespoons olive oil · 2 shallots (green onions), chopped · 2 slices bacon, chopped · ½ bell (green) pepper, chopped · ¼ cup cooked lima beans · ½ cup cooked string beans · ½ pimento, chopped · Salt and pepper

Sauté chicken well in oil, remove and put aside. In same oil, sauté shallots and bacon. Add bell pepper, then lima and string beans and pimento. Cook about 10 minutes, season to taste, and return chicken to the pan. Cover chicken with sautéed vegetables and simmer 5 minutes.
Serves 1.

CHICKEN LIVERS CHAMBERTIN

ARNAUD'S

2 shallots (green onions), chopped · 3 tablespoons olive oil · ½ pound chicken livers · 4 fresh mushrooms, chopped very fine · Salt and white pepper · 2 tablespoons French green peas · ½ tablespoon sherry

Sauté shallots in oil. Add chicken livers and mushrooms and sauté

until livers are cooked. Season to taste, add peas and then sherry. Heat thoroughly in a casserole and serve.
Serves 2.

CHICKEN CLEMENCEAU

ARNAUD'S

1 (1½-pound) spring chicken · 1 stick butter · 1 small can green peas · 2 medium-sized potatoes, diced and fried · 6 mushrooms, diced · 1 clove garlic, minced · 1 sprig parsley, minced

Cut chicken into 8 pieces. Sauté slowly in butter until well browned and cooked through. Add remaining ingredients and sauté 5–10 minutes.
Serves 2.

CHICKEN CREOLE

ANTOINE'S

1 (3½-pound) frying chicken · ¼ cup olive oil · 1 (#2) can tomatoes · 2 tablespoons butter · 1 teaspoon salt · Pepper and cayenne · 1 sprig thyme · 1 tablespoon minced parsley · 1 bay leaf · 3 minced cloves garlic · 1 tablespoon flour · 6 chopped shallots (green onions) or ½ cup minced onion · 5 tablespoons bell (green) pepper · ½ cup white wine

Disjoint chicken and clean well. Sauté in oil, browning on both sides. Simmer tomatoes and 1 tablespoon butter together 10 minutes, stirring occasionally. Add salt and a few grains of pepper and cayenne and simmer 10 minutes. Add thyme, parsley, bay leaf, and garlic and cook 15 minutes, or until sauce is thick. Melt 1 tablespoon butter, blend in flour, and cook until brown. Add shallots or onion and bell pepper and brown slightly. Add wine, stirring constantly until slightly thickened. Combine wine and tomato mixtures and add chicken. Cover and simmer 45 minutes, or until chicken is tender. Serve with steamed rice.
Serves 4–6.

CHICKEN FRICASSEE À LA GERMAINE

ARNAUD'S

1 (1½–2-pound) broiler · 3 tablespoons butter · Salt and pepper · 1 tablespoon flour · 1 egg yolk · 2 tablespoons cream · 1 large onion, sliced very thin · 1 cup white wine · 3 tablespoons chopped parsley

Disjoint broiler and brown lightly in 2 tablespoons butter in a skillet, seasoning with salt and pepper. Remove chicken to a hot platter to keep warm. In the butter remaining in the skillet, make a roux with flour, and then add egg yolk well beaten with cream. Sauté onion in 1 tablespoon butter until tender but not brown and mix with roux. Add chicken and wine, cover, and simmer over low heat until tender—about 40 minutes. Sprinkle with parsley and serve. Serves 2.

BONED BREAST OF CHICKEN ON HAM

PONTCHARTRAIN

3 (6–8-ounce) boned chicken breasts · 6 thin slices baked ham · 3 eggs · 2 teaspoons cream · Bread crumbs · Flour · 5½ sticks butter · ½ cup glace de viande (meat extract) · Lime slices · Water cress

Split breasts in half, put between 2 sheets of waxed paper, and pound with the flat side of a cleaver. Cut slices of ham into the same shape as the pounded breasts. Dip ham slices into eggs beaten with cream, then press ham slices on the halved chicken breasts. Dip the paired ham and chicken in the egg wash, then roll in 4 parts bread crumbs and 1 part flour. Shake off excess crumbs and sauté carefully in 2 sticks melted butter over low heat until browned on both sides. Transfer to a baking dish, reserving the butter. Bake 10 minutes at 350°, basting frequently with the butter. Arrange the chicken breasts on heated individual serving dishes or overlap them on a large platter. Pour around them a sauce made by melting 3½ sticks butter and stirring in glace de viande. Garnish with lime slices and water cress.
Serves 3.

CHICKEN HASH

PONTCHARTRAIN

¾ stick butter · 2 tablespoons flour · 1 quart chicken stock · 2 pieces celery, diced large · 2 medium-sized bell (green) peppers, diced large · 8 button mushrooms, sliced · 1 (5–6 pound) boiled hen · Salt and white pepper · 4 pimentos, diced

Melt ½ stick butter and stir in flour to make a roux. Gradually add chicken stock, stirring constantly, and simmer 10 minutes. Sauté celery, bell peppers, and mushrooms in ¼ stick butter and add to sauce. Pull meat from chicken, cut into large pieces, and add to sauce. Simmer at least 10 minutes, season to taste, and add pimentos. Traditionally, this is served with Grits Soufflé.
Serves 8.

BREAST OF CHICKEN HAWAIIAN

PONTCHARTRAIN

1 boned chicken breast · Flour · Salt and pepper · Butter · 1 cooking spoon Sauce Espagnole · 1 slice toast · 1 grilled pineapple ring · 1 cooking spoon Béarnaise sauce

Dust chicken with flour, season with salt and pepper, and sauté in butter. On a serving plate, place a cooking spoon of Sauce Espagnole. Cover with slice of toast and grilled pineapple ring and top with the cooked chicken breast. Cover with a sharp Béarnaise sauce.
Serves 1.

CHICKEN BREAST MAITLAND

DUNBAR'S

8 whole chicken breasts · Salt and pepper · 1 cup chicken stock · ¼ pound pork sausage · 1 small white onion, chopped · 1 cup chicken stock · 1 teaspoon Kitchen Bouquet · 1 tablespoon flour · ½ tablespoon water · ¼ pound pecans · 2 tablespoons sherry

Season chicken breasts with salt and pepper, put in an open pan

with 1 cup chicken stock, and bake 15 minutes at 350°. Cover pan and steam about 25 minutes.
Cook sausage, remove from pan, and set aside. Brown onion well in sausage grease. Remove onion and add to sausage and chicken stock in a blender. After blending, stir in Kitchen Bouquet and mixture of flour and water for thickening. Add pecans and sherry at the last minute. Serve hot over chicken breasts.
Serves 8.

CHICKEN PONTALBA

BRENNAN'S

1 stick butter · ½ cup thinly sliced white onion · ¼ cup chopped shallots (green onions) · 1 tablespoon minced garlic · ½ cup chopped mushrooms · ½ cup chopped ham · 1 cup diced potato, deep-fried light brown and drained on absorbent paper · ½ cup white wine · 1 tablespoon chopped parsley · 2 pounds chicken leg, thigh, and breast, boned · Seasoned flour · Shortening · 1½ cups Béarnaise sauce · toast triangles · paprika

In a large skillet sauté in butter the onion, shallots, and garlic. Add mushrooms, ham, and potatoes and continue cooking about 5 minutes. Add wine and parsley, cook a few minutes longer, and remove from heat but keep warm. Dredge chicken in seasoned flour and fry until golden brown. Arrange chicken on a bed of ham-mushroom-potato sauce and cover chicken with Béarnaise sauce. Flank with toast triangles and sprinkle lightly with paprika.
Serves 2 or 3.

CHICKEN RIZOTTO FRUITS DE MER

ARNAUD'S

2 shallots (green onions), chopped fine · 2 tablespoons olive oil · 6 boiled shrimp, chopped fine · 4 raw oysters, chopped fine · 4 ounces crabmeat · 1 tablespoon canned tomatoes · Salt and white pepper · 1 cup cooked rice · 1 chicken (broiler) · 1 stick butter · ¼ cup chicken bouillon

Sauté shallots in oil, add seafood, and cook 10 minutes. Add tomatoes

and cook 5 minutes longer. Season to taste and add rice, stirring together well.
Disjoint chicken and sauté in butter. When well browned, add bouillon and season.
To serve, put a large mound of seafood-rice in center of a dish, surround with chicken, and pour over pan juices.
Serves 2.

CHICKEN ROCHAMBEAU

BRENNAN'S

2 (2½-pound) chickens · Seasoned flour · 1½ sticks butter · 1 cup minced shallots (green onions) · 1 teaspoon minced garlic · 2 tablespoons flour · 2 cups chicken stock · ½ cup chopped mushrooms · 1 tablespoon Worcestershire sauce · ½ teaspoon salt · Dash cayenne · ½ cup Burgundy · 4 Holland Rusks · ¼ pound sliced boiled ham · ½ cup Béarnaise sauce

Disjoint and bone chicken, using neck, skin, and bones to make stock. Dredge chicken in seasoned flour and sauté in butter until golden brown and tender. Keep warm in a covered dish. Sauté shallots and garlic in remaining butter. Add flour and brown well. Blend in stock, add mushrooms, and simmer 15 minutes. Add Worcestershire sauce, salt, cayenne, and wine and heat through. Arrange Holland Rusks on a platter and cover with ham slices. Pour chicken sauce over ham, arrange chicken pieces on sauce, and cover with Béarnaise sauce.
Serves 4.

CHICKEN TURENNE

GALATOIRE'S

3 (2-pound) spring chickens · Salt and pepper · 2 sticks butter · 12 ounces broth · ½ pint sherry · 12 artichoke hearts, boiled and sliced · 8 ounces mushrooms, sliced

Disjoint chickens, season with salt and pepper, and fry in butter until brown. Cover with broth and sherry and add artichokes and mushrooms. Simmer about 45 minutes.
Serves 6.

CHICKEN VICTORIA

ARNAUD'S

½ chicken, boned · 4 tablespoons olive oil · ½ raw potato, diced · 2 slices raw bacon, chopped · 4 raw mushrooms, chopped fine · Salt and white pepper · 1 slice toast · ½ cup medium cream sauce · 1 teaspoon capers

Sauté chicken in oil. Remove chicken and sauté potato, bacon, and mushrooms until browned. Return chicken to pan, cover, and simmer 15 minutes. Season to taste and serve on toast topped with hot cream sauce with capers added.
Serves 1.

SUPREME DE VOLAILLE BOURGUIGNONNE

MASSON'S

4 whole boned chicken breasts · Salt and pepper · 1 stick butter · 2 teaspoons olive oil · 1 cup small onions · 8 ounces sliced mushrooms · ⅕ bottle French red Burgundy · 2 shallots (green onions), chopped · ½ cup heavy cream

Season breasts with salt and pepper and sauté in butter and oil. Brown nicely on both sides. Remove chicken breasts and keep them warm. Add onions, sliced mushrooms, and ¼ of wine, cover, and cook about 30 minutes at 350°. Cook shallots in the pan in which breasts were sautéed, until they are soft. Add remaining wine and cook until it reduces to half. Add cream and simmer 2 minutes. Pour over chicken breasts and serve.
Serves 4.

SUPREME DE VOLAILLE EN PAPILLOTE

ARNAUD'S

½ chicken breast, boned · 1 tablespoon olive oil · 1 shallot (green onion), chopped very fine · 3 ounces chopped mushrooms · ½ stick butter · ¼ cup flour · ½ cup chicken stock · Salt and white pepper · 1 tablespoon white wine

Sprinkle chicken breast with oil and broil about 15 minutes. Sauté shallot and mushrooms in butter, stir in flour, and gradually add

chicken stock. Season to taste and add wine. Simmer 5 minutes. Fold parchment paper in half and cut into heart shape. Open and place chicken breast on one half. Cover chicken with sauce, fold over paper, and seal edges all around. Bake in very slow oven until paper is brown.
Serves 1.

SUPREMES DE VOLAILLE EN PAPILLOTE

PONTCHARTRAIN

2 tablespoons butter · 2 boned chicken breasts · 2 ham slices · 1½ cups Italienne Sauce

Fold 2 pieces of parchment in half and cut into heart shapes. Either butter or oil paper well. Quickly brown chicken breasts in butter. In the center of each parchment-paper heart place a slice of ham cut into a triangle. Cover ham with 1 tablespoon of reduced Italienne Sauce. Place the chicken breast on the sauce and cover with more sauce. Close the paper by folding over the chicken and pleating the edges so as to entirely seal in the contents. Put the papillotes in a baking pan and bake at 375° to complete cooking of the chicken, and brown and puff out the papillotes.
Serves 2.

BAKED ROCK CORNISH HEN CUMBERLAND

COMMANDER'S

8 Rock Cornish hens · ½ cup water · Juice of 3 oranges · 1 orange peel, shredded · Juice of 1 lemon · 1 lemon peel, shredded · 1 tablespoon dry mustard · 1 teaspoon ginger · Pinch cayenne pepper · 1 cup Madeira wine · ½ teaspoon salt · 2 cups currant jelly

Bake Rock Cornish hens until golden brown, basting every 8 minutes with ½ cup water added to pan juices. Boil lemon and orange peel in juices until transparent. Mix peel and juices with mustard, ginger, cayenne, wine, salt, and jelly. Heat and serve over Cornish hens.
Serves 8.

CORNISH HEN MARDI GRAS

DUNBAR'S

8 Rock Cornish hens · Salt and pepper · 3 cups chicken stock · 3½ ounces pâté de foie gras · 1 small can truffles, sliced · 2 tablespoons flour · 1 tablespoon water · 1 teaspoon Kitchen Bouquet · 4 ounces Chablis · ½ pound box wild rice

Season hens with salt and pepper and brown in an uncovered pan with 1 cup chicken stock in a 350° oven 25 minutes. Cover pan and steam 20–25 minutes.

Put 2 cups chicken stock in a saucepan and stir in pâté, truffles, mixture of flour and water, and Kitchen Bouquet. Add Chablis just before serving.

Prepare wild rice according to the directions on the package. Cover each serving of wild rice with sauce, top with hens, and pour over remaining sauce.

Serves 8.

ROCK CORNISH HEN FLAMBÉE TWELFTH NIGHT

ARNAUD'S

½ bunch shallots (green onions), chopped fine · ¼ pound chicken livers, chopped fine · 1 bell (green) pepper, chopped fine · ½ pimento, chopped fine · 3 sprigs chopped parsley · 1 clove chopped garlic · 1 cup cooked wild rice · 2 tablespoons butter · 1 egg · Salt and pepper · 2 Rock Cornish hens · 2 ounces pâté de foie gras · 2 ounces rum

Mix together well the shallots, chicken livers, bell pepper, pimento, parsley, garlic, and wild rice and sauté in butter. Add egg, mix well, and stuff hens. Season to taste and bake 25 minutes at 250–300°. Place a portion of pâté de foie gras on the opening of each hen over the stuffing. Pour over rum, ignite, and serve flaming.

Serves 2.

BREAST OF GUINEA HEN WITH CHASSEUR SAUCE

ARNAUD'S

2 shallots (green onions), chopped · 2 tablespoons butter · 2 tablespoons flour · ½ cup beef bouillon · 8 sliced mushrooms · 3 tablespoons brandy · 1 tablespoon white wine · Salt and white pepper · 1 breast of guinea hen, split and broiled

Sauté shallots in butter, stir in flour, and blend in bouillon. Add mushrooms and cook 10 minutes. Add brandy and wine and season to taste. Add breast of guinea hen and cook 15 minutes longer. Serves 2.

PIGEONNEAUX ACADIENS

BRENNAN'S

½ pound chicken livers · ½ pound chicken gizzards · ¼ pound finely chopped ham · 1 bunch shallots (green onions), chopped · 2 tablespoons butter · Salt and pepper · 2 cups French bread, soaked in stock or water and squeezed dry · ¼ bunch parsley, chopped · 4 squabs

Sauté chicken livers, gizzards, ham, and shallots in butter. Season to taste, add the bread, and stir constantly on low heat about 10 minutes. Add parsley.
Roast squabs 30 minutes at 450°. Let cool, then stuff squabs, tie the legs, and return to oven at 450° for 20 minutes more.
Serves 4.

PIGEONNEAUX PARADIS

ANTOINE'S

6 squabs · Salt and pepper · Butter · 1 cup chopped celery · 1 cup chopped carrot · ½ cup chopped onion

SAUCE PARADIS: *½ stick butter · ¼ cup flour · 2 cups double-strength veal stock · ½ cup Madeira wine · 2 tablespoons red currant jelly · 2 cups seedless white grapes · 2 large truffles, sliced*

Sprinkle squabs inside and out with salt and pepper and rub with butter. Spread mixed celery, carrot, and onion on the bottom of a

roasting pan and place squabs on top. Roast about 30 minutes at 325°. Remove squabs from pan to a deep casserole, pour over Sauce Paradis, cover, and bake 15 minutes.
To make sauce: Melt butter, blend in flour, and stir until smooth. Add veal stock (or chicken stock may be substituted), stirring constantly until slightly thickened. Add wine and jelly, stirring until jelly is melted, then add grapes and truffles.
Serves 6.

TERRINE OF PHEASANT ANTOINE*

2 pounds raw ground veal · 3 pounds raw ground pork · 2 pounds raw ground pheasant meat · 2 whole raw eggs · 3 truffles, coarsely chopped · 1 tablespoon salt · 1 tablespoon black pepper · 1 cup cognac · 2 cups shelled pecans, parboiled and drained · 1 pound sliced bacon · 9 (6″×½″×½″) strips cooked ham · 9 (6″×½″×½″) strips raw bacon fat · 9 (6″×½″×½″) strips raw pheasant breast

Combine all ingredients except the last four and mix until well blended—should have the consistency of a meat loaf. Line the bottom of loaf pan (18″×5″×6″) with bacon slices, then cover with 1 inch of stuffing. Lay strips of ham, bacon, and pheasant on top of stuffing, keeping strips ½ inch apart. Alternate layers of stuffing and strips, finishing with a 1-inch layer of stuffing. Cover the top with slices of bacon. Place loaf pan in a shallow pan filled with water and bake about 2 hours at 350°, or until fat rises to top and meat shrinks away from sides of pan. Set aside to cool for several hours and then refrigerate for 12 hours. To serve, unmold from pan, remove excess fat, cut in slices, and serve on plate with cold meat jelly.
Serves 15.

* Created for a dinner of the Chevaliers du Tastevin.

Meat

BEEF FILLET TIPS À LA EUGÈNE EN CASSEROLE WITH NOODLES

ARNAUD'S

6 ounces beef fillet tips · 4 tablespoons olive oil · ½ white onion, chopped fine · 1 tablespoon flour · ½ cup beef bouillon · 2 tablespoons chopped cooked carrots · Salt and Pepper · 2 tablespoons red wine · 4 ounces noodles

Sauté beef in oil with onion about 10 minutes. Stir in flour, then blend in bouillon. Add carrots, season to taste, and add wine. Cover and simmer about 4 minutes. Boil noodles according to the directions on the package and serve with beef tips and sauce in a casserole dish. Serves 2.

MARINATED FILET MIGNON

BRENNAN'S

4 (14-ounce) filets mignon · 6 truffles, sliced · 2 slices bacon, quartered · Salt and pepper · 1 teaspoon crushed peppercorns · 3 bay leaves · ½ teaspoon allspice · 3–6 cloves · 1 cup brandy · 1 cup Burgundy · 1 cup vegetable oil · 1 stick butter · 3 tablespoons flour · 2 cups beef stock · 16 whole mushrooms

Make 2 slits in each filet about 3 inches long and not quite to the underside. Stuff with slices of truffle, bacon, and salt and pepper. Make marinade in a 9″×9″×3″ pan or dish by combining peppercorns, bay leaves, allspice, cloves, brandy, Burgundy, and oil. Place prepared filets in marinade and refrigerate 24 hours or longer. Remove and drain filets and grill according to taste. Melt butter in a saucepan, stir in flour, and brown. Blend in beef stock and 1 cup of marinade. Stir in mushrooms, heat through, and pour over filets. Serves 4.

TOURNEDOS ROSSINI

ANTOINE'S

1 stick butter · 3 tablespoons flour · 2 cups strong beef stock · 1 jigger Madeira wine · Salt and pepper · 6 small tournedos of beef · 6 toast rounds · 6 slices pâté de foie gras

Melt butter, blend in flour, and add beef stock. After cooking to thicken, add Madeira wine. Season tournedos and grill to taste. Place tournedos on toast, top with slice of pâté, and cover with sauce.
Serves 6.

TOURNEDOS ROSSINI

BRENNAN'S

½ stick butter · 1½ tablespoons flour · 1 cup beef stock · 5 peppercorns, crushed · 1 bay leaf · 1 allspice · 1 clove · 2 tablespoons brandy · 2 tablespoons Burgundy · 2 tablespoons vegetable oil · 4 filets mignon · ½ pound pâté of pork liver · Truffles, sliced

Melt butter, blend in flour, and brown. Blend in beef stock, stirring until smooth. Add peppercorns, bay leaf, allspice, clove, brandy, Burgundy, and oil and simmer 5 minutes. Remove bay leaf, allspice, and clove. Broil filets to taste and place on serving plate. Put a slice of pâté on each filet and garnish with truffle slices. Pour hot sauce over all.
Serves 4.

TOURNEDOS ROYAL

BRENNAN'S

¼ cup butter · ½ cup chopped onion · ¼ cup bread crumbs · 1 teaspoon paprika · 1 teaspoon capers · 1 teaspoon chopped truffles · Pinch powdered thyme · 1 cup sweetbreads, parboiled and chopped fine · 4 artichoke hearts · 4 (12–14-ounce) filets mignon · ¼ cup Béarnaise sauce

Melt butter and sauté onion, bread crumbs, paprika, capers, truffles, and thyme. Add sweetbreads and heat through. Divide in 4 portions and roll into balls, placing each ball in an artichoke heart. After seasoning and broiling to taste, put each filet mignon on a serving plate, cover with 1 tablespoon Béarnaise sauce, and top with filled artichoke heart.
Serves 4.

DAUBE CREOLE

DUNBAR'S

¼ pound salt pork fat · 3 bay leaves · 1 bunch thyme · 1 bunch parsley · 3 cloves garlic · 1 large onion · 4 cloves · 2 tablespoons salt · 1 tablespoon pepper · 1 (12–14-pound) boneless beef round · 1 chopped onion · 3 quarts beef stock · 2 cups sherry

Cut salt pork fat into thin strips. Finely chop bay leaves, thyme, parsley, garlic, onion, and cloves and mix with salt and pepper. Roll pork fat strips in seasoned herb mixture. Make cuts in beef round and push seasoned strips into the incisions. Brown the roast in an uncovered dry roasting pan about 30 minutes at 300°. At the end of that time, sprinkle roast with chopped onion, pour over beef stock and sherry, and cook at 350° about 3½ hours. Slice at the table (guests should remove the pockets of seasoning from their slices). Serves 16–18.

LAMB CHOPS MIRABEAU

ARNAUD'S

1 shallot (green onion), chopped fine · 1 tablespoon butter · ½ cup tomatoes · Salt and white pepper · 2 slices toast · 4 lamb chops · ½ cup medium cream sauce · 1 tablespoon capers

Sauté shallot in butter, stir in tomatoes, and cook about 10 minutes. Season to taste. On each serving plate, place tomato sauce, then slice of toast, then broiled lamb chops. Cover with hot cream sauce, to which capers have been added.
Serves 2.

LAMB CHOPS HAWAIIAN FLAMBÉE

ARNAUD'S

2 lamb chops · 2 slices pineapple · 2 maraschino cherries · 2 ounces rum

Broil lamb chops until done and broil pineapple slices until lightly browned. Place pineapple rings on chops with cherries in centers.

Warm the rum and pour it over chops and pineapple, ignite, and serve flaming.
Serves 1.

NOISETTE D'AGNEAU HAWAIIAN
(Côtelette Hawaii)

ANTOINE'S

½ cup Espagnole sauce · ½ cup coulis of ham · ¼ cup chopped shallots (green onions) · 1 (¼-inch) slice fresh pineapple · 1 tablespoon butter · 1 slice raw lamb the thickness of 2 chops cut from a boned rack of lamb · ¼ cup Béarnaise sauce · 1 large fresh whole mushroom, broiled*

Make a good Espagnole sauce (brown sauce) and add to it coulis of ham and shallots cooked together and reduced. Sauté pineapple in butter, place on a hot serving plate, and cover with Espagnole sauce mixture. Cook lamb slice under the broiler until rare, place on top of pineapple, and cover lamb with Béarnaise sauce. Top with hot broiled mushroom.
Serves 1.

* A strong clear broth made with a ham bone or ham scraps.

GRILLADES

DUNBAR'S

6 (6-inch) squares beef sirloin, ½ inch thick · 1 tablespoon shortening · 1 tablespoon flour · 1 onion, chopped · 1 clove garlic, chopped · 4 sprigs thyme, chopped · 2 bay leaves · 1 bell (green) pepper, chopped · 4 sprigs parsley, chopped · 2 medium-sized tomatoes, chopped · 2 cups water · Salt and pepper to taste*

Brown beef lightly in shortening and then remove beef from the skillet. Add flour, onion, garlic, thyme, bay leaves, bell pepper, and

* Veal or beef round may be substituted.

parsley to fat in the skillet and brown thoroughly to make a dark roux. Add tomatoes and water and simmer about 30 minutes. Add beef, season, and simmer about an hour, or until beef is tender. Serve over rice or fried grits.
Serves 6.

VEAL ELMWOOD

1 pound veal fillet · 1 teaspoon salt · ½ teaspoon fresh ground pepper · 1 sliced onion · ½ sliced bell (green) pepper · 1 (2-ounce) can large whole mushrooms · ⅛ cup olive oil · 1 ounce sauterne

Place all ingredients except sauterne in a skillet. Sauté at high heat until veal is lightly browned, about 20 minutes. Add sauterne and sauté at lower heat 10–15 minutes, or until veal is tender.
Serves 4.

VEAL DE MAINTENON, MARCHAND DE VIN

ARNAUD'S

2 slices veal round · Olive oil · 2 slices tomato

DRESSING: *1 tablespoon chopped shallots (green onions) · ¼ pound ground beef · 2 slices stale French bread, squeezed out in water · ½ stick butter · Salt and pepper*

SAUCE: *3 chopped shallots · ¼ cup tomatoes, crushed · ⅛ cup mushroom stems and pieces, chopped fine · ½ tablespoon olive oil · ½ cup brown gravy · ⅛ cup red wine*

Sauté veal lightly in olive oil and cover with dressing. Top with sliced tomato and broil 5 minutes. Pour over marchand de vin sauce before serving.

To make dressing: Sauté shallots, ground meat, and bread in butter 10 minutes. Season to taste.

To make sauce: Sauté shallots, tomatoes, and mushrooms in olive oil. Add gravy and wine and simmer about 10 minutes.
Serves 2.

~~spinach dip~~ artichoke & cream

red bean soup

~~stuffed crab~~ (or)

shrimp a la Orleans in shells.

(or) ~~chicken creole c rice~~

veg

souffled carrots (or)

Tomatoes florentine

bread pudding

HAM STEAK HAWAIIAN WITH SWEET POTATOES AND CHAMPAGNE SAUCE À LA GERMAINE

ARNAUD'S

2 small ham steaks or 1 ham steak, halved · 2 sweet potatoes, boiled, peeled, and halved · Flour · 4 tablespoons oil · 2 slices pineapple · 2 maraschino cherries

SAUCE: *½ white onion, chopped very fine · 2 tablespoons olive oil · 1 tablespoon flour · ¼ tablespoon dry mustard · Pinch salt · ½ cup champagne · 2 tablespoons sugar*

Broil ham steaks. Roll sweet potato halves in flour and fry in oil. Top each ham steak with a lightly broiled pineapple slice with a cherry in the center, and arrange on an ovenproof platter surrounded by sweet potatoes.
To make sauce: Sauté onion in oil, stir in flour, add mustard and salt, and finally add champagne. Pour sauce in the platter with ham steaks and sweet potatoes. Sprinkle sugar over ham and potatoes and run platter under low flame until well heated.
Serves 2.

JAMBALAYA

DUNBAR'S

2 onions, chopped · 4 tablespoons butter · 1 can tomatoes · ½ can tomato paste · 4 cloves garlic, chopped · 2 pieces celery, chopped · ¼ bell (green) pepper, chopped · 1 teaspoon chopped parsley · ½ teaspoon thyme · 3 cloves, chopped · 1 pound boiled ham, diced · 2 pounds shrimp, peeled and boiled · 3 cups cooked rice · Salt, pepper, and cayenne

Sauté onions in butter 5 minutes. Add tomatoes and tomato paste and cook 5 minutes, stirring constantly. Add garlic, celery, bell pepper, parsley, thyme, and cloves. Cook 30 minutes, stirring frequently. Stir in ham and cook 5 minutes. Stir in shrimp and cook 5 minutes. Stir in rice, season to taste, and simmer 30 minutes, stirring often.
Serves 8.
Jambalaya makes a good main dish for supper served with salad and corn bread. It can also be served as a vegetable, decreasing the

amount of ham and shrimp. Although jambalaya is a leftover dish itself (its name is said to mean "clean up the kitchen"—and any odd bits of meat, chicken, or seafood can be added), leftover jambalaya makes a good stuffing for peppers.

CASSOULET TOULOUSIANE

ANTOINE'S

1 package white navy beans · 1 ham bone · 1 (2″×8″) piece bacon rind · Bouquet garni (celery, thyme, parsley, and bay leaf in a cheesecloth) · 1 onion stuck with several cloves · 1 clove garlic · Salt to taste · ½ pound raw pork · ½ pound raw lamb · ½ pound sausage · ½ cup bacon fat · 1 (2-pound) goose · ½ cup minced white onions · ¼ cup minced shallots (green onions) · 3 slices bacon · 1 cup meat stock · Pepper · ¼ cup bread crumbs · ½ stick butter · Salt to taste

Cook beans with ham bone, bacon rind, bouquet garni, onion stuck with cloves, garlic, and salt. Cover with boiling water and cook until beans are done. Do not overcook, as beans must remain whole. Cut the pork, lamb, and sausage into 1-inch pieces and brown well in fat. When meat is browned, pour off fat.

Season goose inside and out and roast in the oven. When goose is cooked, cut into 1-inch pieces and set in a warm place.

In a separate pan cook white onions, shallots, and bacon cut in julienne strips. When onions and bacon are cooked, add to pork, lamb, sausage meat, and cut-up goose. Add meat stock and continue to cook until all meats are tender. Add a little pepper.

Fill the bottom of a large baking pan with a layer of cooked beans. Cover the beans with a layer of cooked meat and cut-up goose. Follow with another layer of beans, continuing to alternate layers until pan is full, ending with beans on top. Sprinkle bread crumbs on last layer of beans and dot with butter. Bake in a very slow oven about 1 hour. Taste for seasoning and serve.

Serves 6.

Vegetables and Salads

LE FOND D'ARTICHAUT AU GRATIN FERMIÈRE*

ANTOINE'S

1 anchovy, minced · 1 cooked heart of artichoke · 1 tablespoon cooked cauliflower · ¼ cup cream sauce · ½ tablespoon grated Swiss cheese · ½ tablespoon bread crumbs

Place anchovy in bottom of artichoke heart. Cover with cauliflower and heat under broiler. Cover with cream sauce and sprinkle with mixed grated cheese and bread crumbs. Brown under broiler and serve.
Serves 1.

* Created for a dinner of the Chevaliers du Tastevin.

ARTICHOKE WITH MUSTARD SAUCE

MASSON'S

2 artichokes · ½ cup mayonnaise · 4 tablespoons Creole mustard

Cook artichokes in salted water until tender. Cut in half lengthwise and clean. Fill the cavity with mixture of mayonnaise and mustard. Can be served hot or cold.
Serves 4.

STUFFED ARTICHOKE

MANALE'S

2 cups bread crumbs · 12 chopped anchovies · 4 pods chopped garlic · ¼ cup chopped parsley · 1 cup grated Parmesan cheese · Salt and pepper · 6 artichokes · ½ pint olive oil

Mix together bread crumbs, anchovies, garlic, parsley, grated cheese, and salt and pepper. Trim stems and tops of artichokes, open leaves, and fill with the above mixture. Pack stuffed artichokes tightly in a pot half filled with water. Pour olive oil over artichokes. Bring to a boil, then simmer covered 45 minutes, or until leaves put out easily.
Serves 6.

AVOCADO À LA MAISON

MASSON'S

4 ripe avocados · Juice of 2 lemons · 1 cup water · 1 cup bread crumbs · 4 tablespoons grated Parmesan cheese · ½ teaspoon garlic powder

Peel avocados and cut into quarters. Soak in mixture of lemon juice and water. Combine crumbs, grated cheese, and garlic and roll avocado quarters in the mixture.
Serves 8.
Can be used as hors d'oeuvre or vegetable.

SOUFFLÉED CARROTS

DUNBAR'S

2 bunches carrots · ½ stick butter, melted · ½ cup sugar · 1 egg · ¼ cup evaporated milk · ⅓ cup flour · 1½ teaspoons cinnamon · 1½ teaspoons baking powder

Peel carrots and slice into thin rings. Boil until tender and mash well. Add melted butter and sugar and beat in egg. Add milk, flour, cinnamon, and baking powder and blend well. Bake in a greased baking dish at 350° 30–50 minutes, or until a knife inserted in the center comes out clean.
Serves 6–8.

SOUFFLÉED CORN

DUNBAR'S

6 ears fresh corn · 1 stick butter · ½ cup sugar · 1 tablespoon flour · ½ cup evaporated milk · 2 eggs, well beaten · 1½ teaspoons baking powder · Melted butter · 1 teaspoon cinnamon · ½ cup sugar · Red cherries and green leaves

Cut corn from ears with a sharp knife or grate it. Melt butter and sugar and add flour slowly. Gradually blend in milk, then add

beaten eggs, then baking powder. Mix all ingredients thoroughly and pour into a greased baking dish. Bake at 350° until brown, about 30–50 minutes. When done, brush with melted butter and sprinkle with mixture of sugar and cinnamon. Garnish with red cherries and green leaves.
Serves 6–8.

BAKED CUSHAW

DUNBAR'S

1 cushaw (or pumpkin) · 2 sticks butter · 2 cups sugar · 1½ cups milk · 4 eggs · ½ teaspoon nutmeg · ½ teaspoon allspice · ¼ teaspoon salt

Wash cushaw well and cut into small pieces. Boil until tender, drain, and scoop pulp from shells. Mash pulp well and blend with all other ingredients. Put mixture in a baking dish and bake until brown, about 30 minutes.
Serves 6–8.

STUFFED EGGPLANT

GALATOIRE'S

1 large eggplant · 2 tablespoons chopped shallots (green onions) · 1 teaspoon parsley · 4 tablespoons butter · Salt and pepper · ½ cup lump crabmeat · ½ cup cooked shrimp (or 1 cup of either) · Bread crumbs · Grated cheese

Cut eggplant lengthwise and bake in oven until tender. Scoop out pulp, being careful to keep skin intact for restuffing. In a skillet brown shallots and parsley in butter. Season and add pulp of eggplant and shrimp and/or crabmeat. Stir together and cook for a few minutes, then stuff into eggplant shells. Sprinkle with bread crumbs and grated cheese and bake in a moderate oven until brown.
Serves 2.

GRITS SOUFFLÉ

PONTCHARTRAIN

8 ounces grits · 1 quart salted water · ¾ pound diced Cheddar cheese · 1 cup breakfast (light) cream · 6 egg yolks

Cook grits in salted water according to the directions on the package. When the grits are done, add cheese. Combine cream with egg yolks, beat well, and then stir into grits. Bake, covered, about 25 minutes at 350°.
Serves 10.

FRIED GRITS

DUNBAR'S

2 cups uncooked hominy grits · Water · Salt · 1 teaspoon baking powder · 7 eggs · 1 stick butter · ½ cup milk · Flour · ½ teaspoon salt · ½ teaspoon sugar · Shortening

Cook grits according to directions on the package, in boiling water with salt and baking powder, for 15 minutes. Whip in 3 beaten eggs, stir in butter, and cook 15 minutes longer. Pour into shallow pan to 1-inch depth and set in the refrigerator overnight. Cut grits into 3-inch squares. Dip squares in a wash of 4 eggs and milk and roll in flour, salt, and sugar mixture until well coated. Fry in shortening until golden brown.
Serves 6.

GUMBO GOUTER

DUNBAR'S

1 tablespoon shortening · 1 large eggplant, peeled · 3 bell (green) peppers · ½ pound okra · 2 large onions · 1 clove garlic · 1 small can tomatoes · ½ teaspoon sugar · Salt pork (optional) · Water to cover · Salt and pepper to taste · Cooked shrimp (optional)

Melt shortening in a saucepan and add all ingredients (except shrimp), cut up. Cover tightly and simmer 1½ hours, stirring often to avoid burning. Add shrimp just before removing from fire.
Serves 6.

MIRLITON FARCI
(Stuffed Vegetable Pears)

DUNBAR'S

4 mirlitons · 1 stick butter · ½ pound ham, chopped fine · 1 pound shrimp, boiled, peeled and chopped · 1 small onion, finely chopped · 2 cloves garlic, minced · 2 sprigs thyme · 2 bay leaves · 1 tablespoon chopped parsley · ½ loaf stale French bread · Salt and pepper to taste · Bread crumbs · Butter · Pimento strips · Parsley sprigs*

Wash mirlitons well and parboil until tender. Cut in half, scoop out centers, and save shells. Mash inner pulp well and put in a skillet with melted butter. Add ham, shrimp, onion, garlic, thyme, bay leaves, and parsley. Simmer 20 minutes. Soak bread (torn into pieces) in water and squeeze dry. Add to mixture in skillet and season to taste. Cook 10 minutes over low flame, stirring constantly. Stuff into mirliton shells, sprinkle with bread crumbs, and dot with butter. Bake at 375° until browned and serve garnished with pimento strips and parsley.
Serves 8.

* Squash may be substituted.

FRESH MUSHROOMS MIRABEAU

ARNAUD'S

8 large mushrooms · 1 shallot (green onion), chopped fine · 1 tablespoon butter · ½ cup tomatoes · Salt and white pepper · 2 slices toast · 1 tablespoon capers · ½ cup medium cream sauce

Boil mushrooms in salted water about 10 minutes. Sauté shallot in butter, stir in tomatoes, and cook about 10 minutes. Season to taste. On each serving plate, place tomato sauce, then toast triangles, then 4 mushrooms on the toast. Stir capers into hot cream sauce and pour over mushrooms.
Serves 2.

OKRA EVANGELINE

BRENNAN'S

1 pound fresh okra, sliced · 2 sticks butter · ½ cup chopped white onion · ½ cup chopped ham · 1 cup fluffy cooked rice · Salt and pepper · 4 medium-sized (preferably Creole) tomatoes

Smother sliced okra in melted butter with onion and ham. When cooked through, add fluffy cooked rice. Season to taste and stuff into hollowed-out tomatoes. Bake 10 minutes at 400°.
Serves 4.

PEAS À LA FRANÇAISE

PONTCHARTRAIN

3 tablespoons butter · 6 tiny spring onions · 5 or 6 leaves lettuce, shredded · ½ teaspoon salt · 1 tablespoon sugar · 3 sprigs parsley · 3 sprigs chervil · 2 generous cups peas (fresh or frozen) · ½ cup water · ½ teaspoon flour

Put 2 tablespoons butter in a saucepan and add onions, lettuce, salt, sugar, parsley and chevril sprigs tied together, and peas. Mix and add water. Bring to a boil, cover tightly, and cook rapidly until peas are almost done. Liquid should be reduced by half. Remove from fire and discard herbs. Cream remaining butter and flour and add to peas. Return to fire, shaking to roll peas until flour-butter mixture is combined with liquid. As soon as it boils again, remove and serve.
Serves 6.

BRABANT POTATOES

COMMANDER'S

3 pounds Idaho potatoes · Shortening · 4 cloves garlic, chopped · 1 stick butter · 2 teaspoons chopped parsley · Salt to taste

Peel and wash potatoes. Cut into small cubes, rinse in cool water, and drain. Fry in deep fat until golden brown and set aside. Sauté garlic in butter, add potatoes and parsley. Mix well and season to taste.
Serves 8.

POMMES BERNY

BRENNAN'S

3 large Irish potatoes, peeled · 1 shallot (green onion), chopped · 2 ounces chopped ham · 5 slices bacon, chopped · 1 truffle, chopped · 2 eggs, separated · Salt and pepper · ½ cup flour · 1 cup bread crumbs · 1 cup sliced almonds

Boil the potatoes, heat in oven until very dry, and then mash them. Sauté shallot, ham, and bacon. Drain off fat and mix onion, ham, bacon, and chopped truffle with the mashed dry potatoes. Add egg yolks, season to taste, and roll into balls. Dip in flour, then in egg white, then bread with mixed bread crumbs and almonds. Deep fry until a crisp golden brown.
Serves 4.

POTATOES MASSON

1½ cups cream · 3 eggs · Salt and pepper · ¾ pound sliced raw potatoes · ¼ cup grated Cheddar cheese

Combine cream and beaten eggs and season with salt and pepper. Lay sliced potatoes in a casserole. Pour cream mixture over potatoes and top with grated cheese. Bake 30–40 minutes at 300°.
Serves 4.

POMMES SOUFFLÉES

ANTOINE'S

2 pounds California potatoes (or 1 potato per person) · 1 deep-fat fryer at moderate temperature · 1 deep-fat fryer at very hot temperature

Peel potatoes and cut into long narrow slices ⅛ inch thick. Put slices in wire basket and wash with cold water to remove excess starch. Dry. Place potato slices, a few at a time, in a frying basket in moderately hot fat. When edges begin to puff slightly, transfer

them to very hot fat and cook until fully puffed and golden brown. Drain on absorbent paper, sprinkle with salt, and serve at once. Serves 6–8.

STUFFED BAKED POTATOES

BRENNAN'S

2 large Idaho potatoes · 4 strips bacon, quartered · ¼ cup chopped shallots (green onions) · 2 tablespoons grated Parmesan cheese · ½ cup sour cream · ½ teaspoon salt · ½ teaspoon white pepper · Butter · Paprika

Scrub potatoes well and bake 1 hour at 400°. Grill bacon pieces until crisp. Drain off bacon fat except for 3 tablespoons. Add shallots and sauté slowly. Cut potatoes in half lengthwise and scoop out inside into a skillet, taking care to retain shells intact. Add cheese, cream, salt, and pepper to potato, shallots, and bacon, mixing and mashing to blend thoroughly. Return skillet to low heat and heat

through. Stuff mixture into potato skins, drizzle with butter, and sprinkle with paprika. Bake 15–20 minutes at 350°.
Serves 2.

SPINACH DUNBAR

4 bunches fresh spinach (or 1½ pounds frozen spinach) · 1 quart water · ¾ teaspoon baking soda · ¾ teaspoon salt · 1 stick butter · 1 teaspoon flour · ¼ can evaporated milk · Salt and pepper · 1 hard-boiled egg, riced

Boil fresh spinach in water with baking soda and salt 8–10 minutes (or cook frozen spinach according to the directions on the package). Drain and chop fine. Melt butter in a saucepan and slowly stir in flour. Gradually blend in milk, add spinach, and mix well. Season to taste and garnish with riced egg.
Serves 6–8.

TOMATOES FLORENTINE

MASSON'S

1 medium-sized onion, chopped fine · ½ stick butter · ½ pound frozen spinach · Salt and pepper · 4 medium-sized tomatoes · Grated Romano cheese

Sauté onion in butter and add cooked, seasoned spinach. Cut top and bottom off tomatoes and scoop out to one half of depth. Fill the cavity with spinach-and-onion mixture. Top with grated cheese and bake 10–12 minutes at 300°.
Serves 4.

PLANTAINS CARAMEL
(Sherried Bananas)

DUNBAR'S

6 plantains or half-ripe bananas · Shortening · 1 cup sugar · 2 cups water · 3 cloves · ½ lemon, sliced · ¼ cup butter · 2 tablespoons sherry

Cut plantains or bananas in half lengthwise. Fry in shortening until golden brown and remove from skillet. Brown sugar in skillet.

Add water and cook until it forms a thick syrup. Add cloves, lemon, butter, and sherry and simmer 10 minutes. Add bananas and simmer 5 minutes.
Can be served as a vegetable—excellent as a meat accompaniment, or as a dessert with ice cream.
Serves 6.

SWEET POTATOES HAWAIIAN

DUNBAR'S

6 sweet potatoes · 1/3 cup white sugar · 1/4 pound butter · 3/4 cup crushed pineapple · 1 teaspoon cinnamon · 1/2 cup chopped pecans · Pineapple juice · 1/3 cup brown sugar · Butter

Wash potatoes well, cut in half, and boil until tender, about 30 minutes. Scoop pulp out of shells, reserving shells, and mash well. Add white sugar, butter, pineapple, and cinnamon. Cream mixture and stir in pecans. After dipping shells in pineapple juice, spoon mixture into shells. Top with brown sugar, dot with butter, and bake at 350° until piping hot, about 15 minutes.
Serves 6–12.

YAMS RICHARD

BRENNAN'S

3 pounds yams · 1/4 teaspoon nutmeg · 1/4 teaspoon cinnamon · 1/2 stick butter · 1/2 cup light cream · 1/3 cup chopped pecans · 1/3 cup seedless raisins · 16 marshmallows

Boil yams until tender. Peel and mash, then add nutmeg, cinnamon, melted butter, cream, pecans, and raisins, mixing thoroughly. Place in a buttered 2-quart casserole. Cover the top with marshmallows and bake 25–30 minutes at 350°.
Serves 6.

SALADE DES CHAMPS*

ANTOINE'S

1 bunch water cress · 2 Belgian endive · 1 pink-meat grapefruit

DRESSING: *4 parts olive oil · 1 part white vinegar · Salt and pepper to taste · Dash Tabasco sauce · Dash Lea & Perrins Sauce · Pinch dry mustard mixed with a little vinegar*

Wash salad greens well and drain off all moisture. Separate leaves of endive. Cut grapefruit in half and remove segments. Place grapefruit segments and greens in salad bowl and pour over French dressing made by mixing ingredients listed above. Mix well and serve immediately.
Serves 4.

* Created for a dinner of the Chevaliers du Tastevin.

JACKSON SALAD

BRENNAN'S

¼ head lettuce · Romaine · Chicory · 4 strips crisp bacon · 2 hard-boiled eggs, coarsely chopped · 1 small avocado, diced · Oil · Vinegar · Dry mustard · Salt and black and white pepper

Fill bottom of a salad bowl with mixed greens—lettuce, romaine, and chicory. Mix with greens the crisp crumbled bacon, hard-boiled eggs (holding some aside to sprinkle on top), and avocado.
Make French dressing by combining and shaking well together the oil, vinegar, mustard, salt and pepper. Add some to salad (but do not drench) and place in refrigerator until ready to serve, so that dressing will seep through the salad.
Serves 2.

SALADE RÉGENCE

ARNAUD'S

1 piece celery, chopped fine · Lettuce · 5 slices grapefruit · 5 slices orange · 2 tablespoons mayonnaise · Dash oil and vinegar

Mix chopped celery with a few pieces of lettuce, slices of grapefruit and orange. Add mayonnaise, oil and vinegar. Mix all together well and serve on a leaf of lettuce.
Serves 1.

THOUSAND ISLAND RING

PONTCHARTRAIN

2 tablespoons gelatin · ½ cup cold water · 1 cup chili sauce · 1½ cups mayonnaise · 6 hard-boiled eggs, diced · 1 can pimentos, diced · ½ teaspoon sugar · Dash Tabasco sauce · 1 teaspoon Worcestershire sauce · 1 cup celery, diced

Soak gelatin in cold water, then stir over hot water until dissolved. Mix the remaining ingredients and add to gelatin. Pour into an oiled ring mold and chill until firm. Invert on a bed of lettuce and fill the center with seafood (shrimp, crab, or lobster). Serve with Russian dressing and Melba toast.
Serves 8.

Sauces and Dressings

BÉARNAISE SAUCE

BRENNAN'S

4 egg yolks · Juice of 1 lemon · 4 sticks butter · Salt and pepper · 2 tablespoons capers · ¼ cup chopped parsley · 1 tablespoon tarragon vinegar

Beat egg yolks and lemon juice in top of double boiler. Cook slowly over very low heat, never allowing water to come to a boil. Melt butter and add slowly, stirring constantly with a wooden spoon. Add salt and pepper to taste and stir in capers, parsley, and vinegar.
Makes 2 cups.

BÉCHAMEL SAUCE

PONTCHARTRAIN

1 tablespoon butter · 2 tablespoons flour · 2 cups milk · 1 thin slice onion · 1 sprig parsley · 1 tablespoon cream · 1 egg yolk · Pepper · ¼ cup grated Gruyère cheese

Melt butter in a small, heavy-bottomed saucepan. Stir in flour and cook slowly, stirring constantly to prevent turning color. Scald milk with onion and parsley and add to butter-and-flour roux, stirring briskly with a sauce whisk. Bring to a boil and cook slowly 5 minutes. If the sauce seems too thick, add a little more milk. Remove and add cream and egg yolk, beaten together. Season with pepper, strain, and add grated cheese.
Makes about 2¼ cups.

BROWN SAUCE (Quick Method)

PONTCHARTRAIN

1½ tablespoons clarified butter · 1½ tablespoons flour · 2 cups strong brown stock or beef consommé*

Melt butter in a saucepan and blend in a generous 1½ tablespoons

* To clarify butter, heat to melt, skim off pure butter, and discard remaining water.

flour. Cook slowly over a low flame, stirring occasionally, until thoroughly blended and the color of brown wrapping paper. Moisten gradually with brown stock or consommé, bring to a boil, and cook 3–5 minutes, stirring constantly. Lower the flame and simmer gently 30 minutes, stirring occasionally. Skim off fat and strain the sauce through a fine sieve.
Makes about 2 cups.

CREAM SAUCE

BRENNAN'S

1 stick butter · ½ cup flour · 1½ cups milk · ¾ teaspoon salt · ¼ teaspoon cayenne

Melt butter and stir in flour, blending well without browning. Gradually stir in milk and add salt and cayenne, stirring constantly until thickened.
Makes 2 cups.

HEAVY CREAM SAUCE

PONTCHARTRAIN

1 stick butter · 1 heaping cooking spoon flour · 1 quart milk · 2 egg yolks · 1 ounce dry white wine · 1 teaspoon salt

Combine butter and flour and cook until flour has a tint. Add milk which has been scalded, stir until smooth, and simmer at least 5 minutes on a slow fire. Combine egg yolks and wine and beat until smooth. Remove sauce from fire and blend with yolks and wine, adding salt.
Makes about 4¾ cups.

CREOLE SAUCE

COMMANDER'S

2 cups diced onions · 2 cups diced celery · 4 cloves garlic · 2 cups chopped bell (green) peppers · 4 tablespoons olive oil · 3 pounds canned tomatoes, crushed · 1 cup water · 2 bay leaves · ¼ teaspoon thyme · 4 tablespoons chopped parsley · Salt and pepper to taste · 1 tablespoon cornstarch

Sauté onion, celery, garlic, and peppers in olive oil. Add tomatoes, water, and all other ingredients except cornstarch and simmer about 1 hour. Thicken with cornstarch.
Serves 8.
This sauce can be served with chicken, shrimp, or fish, sautéed and added to sauce 20 minutes before serving.

ESPAGNOLE SAUCE
(Brown Sauce)

ANTOINE'S

*½ cup bacon drippings · 1 carrot, coarsely chopped · 2 onions, coarsely chopped · ½ cup flour · 2 quarts brown stock**
A faggot made by tying together the following:
2 stalks celery · 2 sprigs parsley · Pinch of thyme · 1 bay leaf

1 clove garlic · 10 peppercorns · ¼ cup tomato sauce

Melt fat in a heavy saucepan, add carrot and onions, and cook until they start to turn golden. Add flour and cook, stirring frequently, until flour takes on a nice hazelnut brown color. Add 3 cups boiling brown stock, the faggot, garlic, and peppercorns. Cook and stir until the mixture thickens, then add 3 more cups stock. Cook very slowly, stirring occasionally, until the mixture is reduced to about 3 cups. This should take 1–1½ hours. As it cooks, the fat will rise to the surface and should be skimmed off. Add the tomato sauce and cook a few minutes longer. Strain through a fine sieve. Add remaining 2 cups of stock and continue cooking until the sauce is

* Brown stock made with beef bones, onions, carrots, thyme, bay leaf, salt, pepper, and water, simmered 2 hours, and strained.

reduced to 4 cups. Strain and cool, stirring occasionally. Will keep a week stored in the refrigerator with a little melted fat on top. Makes 4 cups.

HOLLANDAISE SAUCE

BRENNAN'S

4 egg yolks · 2 tablespoons lemon juice · 2 sticks butter, melted · ¼ teaspoon salt · Salt and pepper

Beat egg yolks and stir in lemon juice. Cook very slowly in the top of a double boiler, never allowing the water in the bottom to come to a boil. Melt butter and add gradually, stirring constantly with a wooden spoon. Add salt, further season to taste, and continue cooking slowly until thickened.
Makes 1 cup.

RICH HOLLANDAISE SAUCE

PONTCHARTRAIN

5 egg yolks · ¼ cup wine tarragon vinegar · Dash Tabasco sauce · 4 sticks butter, melted · Salt to taste · ⅛ cup tepid water

Combine in a stainless-steel mixing bowl the egg yolks, vinegar, and Tabasco sauce. Whip until very frothy, and while continuing to whip, gradually add melted butter (heated to 200°) in the manner of making mayonnaise. When butter has been blended, season and add water to rectify consistency.
Makes approximately 3 cups.

ITALIENNE SAUCE

PONTCHARTRAIN

1 shallot (green onion), finely chopped · 1 ounce dry white wine · 1 teaspoon chicken base · 1 cup heavy cream sauce*

Combine shallot and white wine and simmer approximately 2 minutes. Add chicken base and cream sauce.
Makes about 1⅛ cups.

* An extract, available in jars.

MADEIRA SAUCE

ANTOINE'S

1 (3-ounce) glass Madeira wine · 1 cup brown sauce · 1 teaspoon concentrated beef drippings · 2 tablespoons butter · 2 tablespoons Madeira wine

This sauce should be made in the same pan in which you have broiled your meat. First remove meat, pouring off all of the fat but retaining meat drippings. Add glass of Madeira (or sherry) and cook, stirring in all the juices which cling to the pan. Cook until the wine is reduced to half the original quantity. Add brown sauce and concentrated beef drippings. Cook 5–10 minutes, then add butter, stirring and mixing everything well together. Do *not* let sauce boil after adding butter. When butter is melted, add 2 tablespoons Madeira and serve over meat, chicken, ham, etc.
Makes 1½–2 cups.

SAUCE MAISON D'OR

ANTOINE'S

1 cup sliced fresh mushrooms · ½ stick butter · 1 cup sliced cooked sweetbreads · 1 cup sliced cooked turkey or chicken breast · 1 truffle, sliced · ½ cup whole blanched cockscombs · ½ cup mushroom water · 1 ounce sherry · 1 cup cream sauce · Salt and pepper to taste · Pinch of nutmeg · 1 egg yolk · ½ cup cream*

Put sliced fresh mushrooms in a pan with butter. Add sliced cooked sweetbreads, slices of turkey or chicken breast cut into strips julienne fashion, sliced truffle, and cockscombs. Cook all of these ingredients for a few minutes and add mushroom water and sherry. Cook a little longer and add cream sauce. Stir well until everything is blended and season with salt and pepper and a pinch of nutmeg. When ready to serve, add a liaison—which is a mixture of egg yolk and cream. This gives the dish a golden color and delicate flavor. Do *not* cook sauce

* A French import, available in gourmet food stores.

after adding egg-yolk-and-cream mixture. Serve over chicken, steak, or lamb chops.
Serves 6.

MARCHAND DE VIN SAUCE

BRENNAN'S

¾ cup butter · ⅓ cup finely chopped mushrooms · ½ cup minced ham · ⅓ cup finely chopped shallots (green onions) · ½ cup finely chopped onion · 2 tablespoons minced garlic · 2 tablespoons flour · ½ teaspoon salt · ⅛ teaspoon pepper · Dash cayenne · ¾ cup beef stock · ½ cup red wine

Melt butter and lightly sauté mushrooms, ham, shallots, onion, and garlic. When onion is golden brown, add flour, salt, pepper, and cayenne. Brown well, about 7–10 minutes, blend in the stock and wine and simmer over low heat 35–45 minutes.
Makes 2 cups.

MARCHAND DE VIN SAUCE

COMMANDER'S

2 tablespoons flour · ½ cup olive oil · 5 cloves minced garlic · 1 bunch shallots (green onions), chopped · 2 tablespoons chopped parsley · 1 cup sliced mushrooms · 1 tablespoon B.V. (beef extract) · 2 cups water · 6 ounces red wine · Salt and pepper to taste

Brown flour in olive oil. Add garlic and shallots. Cook 3 minutes. Add all other ingredients and cook for 10 minutes.
Serves 8.

MONTAUBON SAUCE

ARNAUD'S

1 shallot (green onion), chopped fine · 2 tablespoons olive oil · 2 tablespoons flour · ½ cup beef bouillon · 2 sliced cepes · 3 sliced mushrooms · 8 cooked new potato (tiny) balls · Salt and white pepper*

* A special type of mushroom available in specialty food shops.

Sauté shallot in oil. Blend in flour, then add bouillon. When well blended, add cepes, mushrooms, and potatoes and cook 10 minutes. Season to taste and serve over steak.
Serves 2.

SAUCE MORNAY

PONTCHARTRAIN

*2 ounces grated Parmesan cheese · 1 cup heavy cream sauce · 1 ounce artichoke liquor**

* Water from boiling artichoke with lemon and salt.

Combine half of grated Parmesan cheese with cream sauce and artichoke liquor. Simmer at least 5 minutes and sprinkle remaining cheese over the top.
Makes about 1¼ cups.

ORLEANAISE SAUCE

ARNAUD'S

1 white onion, chopped fine · 2 pieces celery, chopped fine · 1 clove garlic, chopped fine · ½ stick butter · 2 cups tomatoes, cut fine · Dash Worcestershire sauce · Salt and pepper

Sauté onion, celery, and garlic in butter 10 minutes. Add tomatoes and Worcestershire sauce and season to taste. Simmer for 10 minutes and serve over steak.
Makes about 2 cups.

PROVENÇALE SAUCE

COMMANDER'S

5 tablespoons flour · ½ cup olive oil · 3 gloves garlic, chopped · 2 shallots (green onions), chopped · 4 ounces sliced mushrooms · 1 bay leaf · 6 ounces claret · 1 pint water · 1 tablespoon B.V. (beef extract) · ½ cup tomato sauce · 2 tablespoons chopped parsley

Make a brown roux with flour and oil, add garlic, and cook until half browned. Add shallots, mushrooms, and bay leaf. After cooking 3 minutes, add claret, water, B.V., tomato sauce, and parsley. Simmer 20 minutes. Serve over any seafood.
Serves 6.

RICHELIEU SAUCE

ARNAUD'S

2 tablespoons butter · 2 shallots (green onions), chopped fine · 8 sweetbreads, sliced · 8 cepes · 5 whole mushrooms · ¼ cup sherry · 1 cup brown gravy or stock · Salt and pepper*

Sauté in butter 5 minutes the shallots, sweetbreads, cepes, and mushrooms. Add sherry and gravy or stock. Season to taste and let simmer 3 minutes. Serve over steak.
Serves 2–4.

* A special type of mushroom available in specialty food shops.

TOMATO SAUCE

ANTOINE'S

3 tablespoons butter · 1 carrot, coarsely chopped · 1 onion, coarsely chopped · ½ cup flour · 2½ cups canned tomatoes · 1½ cups chicken stock (made with bones, feet and neck) · 2 cloves crushed garlic
A faggot, made by tying together the following:
3 sprigs parsley · 2 stalks celery · Pinch of thyme · 1 bay leaf

Salt and pepper to taste · 2 tablespoons caramelized sugar · Sherry

Melt butter in a heavy saucepan. Add carrot and onion and cook until onion is soft but not brown. Add flour and cook, stirring from time to time, until flour starts to turn golden. Add remaining ingredients except sugar and sherry, bring to a boil, and cook until thickened. Cook slowly 1½–2 hours, or until sauce is reduced to

about 1 pint, stirring occasionally and skimming surface when necessary. Caramelize sugar by cooking equal parts sugar and water until golden brown. Add caramelized sugar, remove faggot, and strain the sauce. Bring to a boil again and cook 5 minutes. Store in a jar, covering top with sherry. Can be kept for a week.
Makes about 1 pint.

EGG DRESSING

COMMANDER'S

3 hard-boiled eggs, chopped fine · 1 cup mayonnaise · 2 tablespoons French mustard · 2 tablespoons lemon juice · 1/4 teaspoon Tabasco sauce

Mix all ingredients together thoroughly and chill well.
Makes 1 pint.

FRENCH DRESSING

COMMANDER'S

1 small onion · 1 clove garlic · 2 whole raw eggs · 3/4 cup oil · 3/4 cup vinegar · 3 tablespoons paprika · 1 tablespoon yellow mustard · 1 teaspoon salt

Chop onion and garlic extremely fine. Mix with eggs, oil, vinegar, paprika, mustard, and salt. Blend well, strain, and serve.
Makes 1 pint.

FRENCH DRESSING

PONTCHARTRAIN

3 teaspoons salt · 3 teaspoons sugar · 1 1/2 teaspoons dry mustard · 1 teaspoon black pepper · 1/2 teaspoon cayenne · 1/2 quart cider vinegar · 1 1/2 quarts salad oil · 1 clove garlic

Combine all ingredients except garlic and shake well or blend in a blender. Place in a jar with garlic to store.
Makes 2 quarts.

REMOULADE SAUCE

BRENNAN'S

¾ cup minced parsley · ¾ cup minced shallots · ¾ cup minced celery · ¾ cup minced dill pickle · 1 tablespoon minced garlic · 1¾ cups Creole (hot) mustard · 3 tablespoons horseradish · ¼ cup vinegar · ¼ cup salad oil

Mix all ingredients together and chill. This sauce will keep, refrigerated, for many weeks. The longer it stands, the better it tastes. For Shrimp Remoulade, marinate 6 large boiled shrimp in ½ cup sauce for each serving. Serve on a bed of shredded lettuce.
Makes about 5 cups.

REMOULADE SAUCE

COMMANDER'S

2 chopped hard-boiled eggs · 2 teaspoons salt · 4 tablespoons paprika · ½ cup Creole (hot) mustard · 1½ pints Wesson Oil *· ½ cup vinegar · 1 lemon · ½ cup chopped celery · 3 cloves garlic, minced · ⅛ bunch parsley, chopped · ½ cup chopped shallots (green onions) · ½ cup tomato catsup · 3 bay leaves ·* Tabasco *sauce to taste*

Put eggs, salt, paprika, and Creole mustard in a mixing bowl. Add oil slowly, thinning with vinegar after the mixture thickens. Cut lemon into quarters, squeeze juice into sauce, and drop in rind. Add remaining ingredients and let set for 6 hours in the refrigerator. Remove lemon rind and bay leaves before serving. This sauce is popularly served with shrimp. In the amount of sauce above, marinate about 50 medium-sized peeled, boiled, and deveined shrimp 2 or 3 hours. Serve on a bed of chopped lettuce garnished with a quartered hard-boiled egg, parsley, or water cress. The sauce can also be used on lump crabmeat, stuffed tomatoes or avocados, or as a dip.
Makes about 1½ quarts.

REMOULADE SAUCE

GALATOIRE'S

1 bunch shallots (green onions) · 1 stalk celery · 2 cloves garlic · 1 sprig parsley · 5 tablespoons Creole (hot) mustard · 2 tablespoons paprika · Salt and pepper · ⅓ cup vinegar · ⅔ cup olive oil

Grind or mince very fine the onions, celery, garlic, and parsley. Add mustard, paprika, salt and pepper. Add vinegar and mix thoroughly, then gradually add olive oil. Refrigerate. Marinate boiled, peeled shrimp in this sauce and serve on shredded lettuce with a garnish of tomato wedges.
Makes 1 quart.

REMOULADE SAUCE

MASSON'S

½ cup chopped celery · ¼ cup chopped parsley · ¼ cup chopped onion · 1 cup cottonseed oil · 2 teaspoons Lea & Perrins Sauce · ¼ cup malt vinegar · ½ cup Creole (hot) mustard · ¼ cup horse-radish · ¼ cup paprika · 2 teaspoons salt · 1 teaspoon black pepper · 1 quart mayonnaise

Combine ingredients as listed. Stir into mayonnaise and mix thoroughly. Keep refrigerated.
Yields 1½ quarts.
Although most commonly served on cold boiled shrimp, this sauce can also be served on tomatoes, head lettuce, as a salad dressing, or over cold lobster or crabmeat.

REMOULADE SAUCE

PONTCHARTRAIN

1 quart salad oil · 1 tablespoon dry mustard · 1 tablespoon yellow mustard · 2 tablespoons paprika · 2 tablespoons horseradish · 2 tablespoons finely chopped parsley · 1 large bell (green) pepper, finely chopped · 2 pieces celery, finely chopped · 2 dill pickles, finely chopped · 4 shallots (green onions), finely chopped · ½ cup wine tarragon vinegar · 2 teaspoons Worcestershire sauce · 1 teaspoon Tabasco sauce · 2 tablespoons salt · 1 teaspoon sugar · 4 pounds shrimp

Gradually add oil (as in making mayonnaise) to dry mustard, yellow mustard, paprika, and horseradish. Add parsley, bell pepper, celery, pickles, and shallots and then add remaining ingredients. Peel and devein boiled shrimp and marinate in sauce, covered in refrigerator, for not less than 48 hours. Will keep, refrigerated, for at least a week. Serves 12.

THOUSAND ISLAND DRESSING

PONTCHARTRAIN

1 cup mayonnaise · ¼ cup chili sauce · 2 tablespoons sweet relish · 2 tablespoons chopped ripe olives · 1 minced pimento · Juice of ½ lemon · Dash Worcestershire sauce · Dash Tabasco sauce

Combine and blend all ingredients.
Makes 1 pint.
Add 2 ounces Beluga caviar for Russian dressing.

VINAIGRETTE DRESSING

COMMANDER'S

¾ cup vinegar · ½ cup Wesson Oil · ½ cup finely chopped shallots (green onions) · 2 tablespoons chopped pimentos · 1 large pickle, chopped fine · 2 tablespoons chopped parsley · 1½ tablespoons paprika · 1 tablespoon salt

Mix all ingredients together well.
Makes 1 pint.

Desserts

BRANDIED FRUIT

DUNBAR'S

1 cup canned peach slices · 1 cup canned apricot slices · 1 cup canned pineapple chunks · 12 red maraschino cherries, chopped · 12 green maraschino cherries, chopped · 1 pinch cinnamon · 3 ounces brandy

Pour off all fruit juice and save for sauce. Dissolve cinnamon in a bit of water and add to juices. Add brandy and stir well. Pour over fruit (fresh strawberries can be added in season) and marinate overnight. Serve in parfait glasses.
Serves 6.

BRANDIED FRUIT THAIS

PONTCHARTRAIN

4 peaches · 4 apricots · 4 pears · 4 pineapple rings · 2 bananas · 2 cups pitted Bing cherries · ½ cup sherry · 1 pound brown sugar · ½ pound shredded blanched almonds · 12 macaroons, crumbled · ½ pound butter · 2 ounces brandy

Marinate diced fruit at least 2 hours in sherry and half of brown sugar. Drain and arrange fruit in layers in a baking dish. Sprinkle each layer with brown sugar, almonds, macaroons, and dabs of butter. Cover the top with crushed macaroon crumbs and bake 10–15 minutes at 350°. When ready to serve, flame with brandy.
Serves 12.

BRANDY BREAD PUDDING

COMMANDER'S

3 cups cubed bread · ½ cup raisins · ½ cup canned mixed fruit cocktail · 1¼ quarts milk · 4 eggs · 1½ cups sugar · 2 tablespoons vanilla · 1 tablespoon butter

Place bread, raisins, and fruit in a baking dish. Let milk come to a boil. Mix eggs, sugar, and vanilla in a dish, pour milk over them, and beat thoroughly. Pour this mixture over bread, raisins, and fruit, dot with butter, and bake at 300° until firm. Serve hot or cold.

SAUCE: *2 cups hot milk · 2 eggs · ¾ cup sugar · 6 tablespoons cornstarch · 2 teaspoons butter · 2 teaspoons vanilla · ½ cup brandy or whiskey (optional)*

Let milk come to a boil. Mix eggs, sugar, cornstarch, and butter in a double boiler, pour milk over them, and cook on slow fire until thickened. Remove, add vanilla and brandy to taste before serving with Bread Pudding.
Serves 6.

CRÊPES SUZETTES

BRENNAN'S

2 eggs · ¾ cup sifted flour · 1 teaspoon sugar · Pinch of salt · Milk

Mix together eggs, flour, sugar, and salt. Add milk until the batter is the consistency of condensed milk, beating until smooth. Heat a 6-inch skillet that has been oiled with vegetable oil. Pour about 2 tablespoons of the batter into skillet, tilting to distribute the batter evenly. Brown the crêpe on both sides, remove, and keep warm in a towel. Re-oil the skillet with a pastry brush and repeat until the batter is used up.

½ stick butter · ¼ cup sugar · Peel of 3 oranges in thin slivers · Peel of 1 lemon in thin slivers · Juice of 1 orange · Juice of ½ lemon · ¾ ounce cointreau · ¾ ounce Grand Marnier · 2 ounces brandy

Melt butter in a chafing dish, add sugar, and mix well. Add orange and lemon peels and juices. Simmer until peels are transparent. Place 3 crêpes at a time in this sauce and fold in halves and quarters, repeating until 12 crêpes are in the chafing dish. Pour over the cointreau and Grand Marnier, and then the brandy. Ignite, tipping slightly. Level the pan and move backward and forward until the flame dies down. Serve 3 crêpes per person, spooning some of the liquid over each portion.
Serves 4.

CRÊPES FITZGERALD

BRENNAN'S

4 crêpes · 4 heaping teaspoons Philadelphia cream cheese · 4 tablespoons sour cream · 3 pats butter · 1 cup frozen strawberries · 3 teaspoons sugar** · 1 jigger strawberry liqueur · 1½ jiggers kirsch*

Have Philadelphia cream cheese and sour cream at room temperature. Mix together, roll in warm crêpes, and put on dessert plates, 2 to a serving. Melt butter in a chafing dish, add strawberries and sugar, and simmer. Pour over strawberry liqueur and kirsch, ignite, and flame. When flame burns out, pour over crêpes and serve.
Serves 2.

* See recipe for Crêpes Suzettes.
** Six teaspoons if fresh strawberries are used.

To make for 4, double crêpes, cream cheese, sour cream, strawberries, and sugar. No extra butter or strawberry liqueur should be added, but increase kirsch to 2 jiggers.

CRÊPES 417

BRENNAN'S

2 crêpes · Chopped fruit and nuts in rum · 2 pats butter ·*

1 teaspoon sugar · Peel of ½ lemon · Peel of 1 orange · Juice of ½ lemon · Juice of 1 orange · ¼ ounce Grand Marnier · ¼ ounce Cherry Heering

Fill warm crêpes with chopped fruit and nuts soaked in rum and place on a dessert plate. Melt butter in a chafing dish and add sugar, lemon peel and juice, and orange peel and juice. Simmer, then add Grand Marnier and Cherry Heering. Ignite and flame. When flame dies, pour over crêpes.
Serves 1.

* See recipe for Crêpes Suzettes.

CRÊPES SOUFFLÉ

PONTCHARTRAIN

CRÊPES: *2 eggs · ¼ pound flour · 1 teaspoon melted butter · ½ pint milk · 1 tablespoon vanilla*

MERINGUE: *6 egg whites · ½ pound powdered sugar · 1 teaspoon grated orange peel · ½ teaspoon egg-shade food coloring · 1 teaspoon liquid pistachio*

SAUCE: *6 egg yolks · ½ pound granulated sugar · ½ pint milk · ¼ pint breakfast (light) cream · ½ teaspoon mace · 4 ounces Jamaica rum*

CRÊPES:
Beat eggs very well and add flour, butter, milk, and vanilla, stirring until smooth. Strain through a very fine sieve. Pour 1½ ounces into a hot, lightly greased frying pan, rotating pan until the surface is completely covered. Cook 2 minutes on each side.

MERINGUE:
Put egg whites in electric mixer and mix slowly about 3 minutes. Add powdered sugar slowly and then beat rapidly for 10 minutes. Add orange peel, food coloring, and pistachio and mix well. Spread 6 crêpes on a table and divide meringue equally in the center of each crêpe. Fold crêpe forward, keeping the meringue inside, and then fold in half. Place crêpes in a buttered pan and bake about 5 minutes at 450°.

SAUCE:
Put egg yolks in a double boiler. Add granulated sugar and stir until smooth. Stir in milk, cream, and mace and cook until slightly thicker than cream. Add the rum just before serving. Pour over individual crêpes.
Serves 6.

CRÊPES ELIZABETH

PONTCHARTRAIN

8 crêpes · 16 tablespoons sliced and sugared strawberries · 1 cup blanched, shredded, slightly toasted almonds · Whipped cream

Make crêpes according to Crêpes Soufflé recipe. Put 2 tablespoons of strawberries on each crêpe and roll to enclose the filling. Arrange the rolls side by side in a shallow buttered baking dish. Sprinkle with almonds and put under broiler until crêpes blister. Serve hot with whipped cream, sweetened and flavored to taste.
Serves 4.

CRÊPES WITH TOASTED ALMONDS

PONTCHARTRAIN

½ cup apricot preserves · ½ stick butter · 2 ounces orange curaçao · 8 crêpes · ½ pound slivered almonds, toasted*

Combine preserves, butter, and curaçao in a saucepan and cook until thickened. Fold crêpes twice, place on a silver platter, and heat 5 minutes in 350° oven. Pour sauce over crêpes and sprinkle with almonds.
Serves 4.

* See recipe for crêpes in Crêpes Soufflé.

CRÊPES WITH APPLE JELLY

PONTCHARTRAIN

1 stick butter · ½ pound powdered sugar · 1 tablespoon grated orange rind · 1 teaspoon brandy · 1 teaspoon pistachio flavoring · 8 crêpes · ½ cup apple jelly · 2 ounces sherry*

Cream butter, sugar, orange rind, brandy, and pistachio flavoring. Divide among 8 crêpes, fill, roll, place on silver platter, and heat 5

* See recipe for crêpes in Crêpes Soufflé.

minutes at 350°. Combine apple jelly and sherry, cook until thickened, pour over crêpes, and serve.
Serves 4.

CRÊPES WITH COTTAGE CHEESE

PONTCHARTRAIN

*¾ cup cottage cheese · ⅓ cup sugar · 1 teaspoon cinnamon · 1 teaspoon vanilla · 8 crêpes**

SAUCE: *3 egg yolks · ¼ cup sugar · 1 teaspoon cornstarch · 1 teaspoon mace · ½ cup light cream · 1 cup milk · 2 ounces rum*

Mix cottage cheese, sugar, cinnamon, and vanilla. Divide among 8 crêpes, fill, fold, and arrange on a silver platter. Heat 5 minutes in a 350° oven and serve with the following sauce.
Combine egg yolks, sugar, and cornstarch and beat until smooth. Add mace, cream, and milk and mix well. Cook over hot water until thickened, stir in rum, and pour over warm crêpes.
Serves 4.

* See recipe for crêpes in Crêpes Soufflé.

CRÊPES WITH CURRANT JELLY

PONTCHARTRAIN

8 crêpes · ½ stick butter · ½ cup red currant jelly · 1 ounce kirsch · 2 ounces red wine*

Fold crêpes, place on silver platter, and warm 5 minutes in 350° oven. Combine butter, jelly, kirsch, and wine, cook until thickened, pour over crêpes, and serve.
Serves 4.

* See recipe for crêpes in Crêpes Soufflé.

CRÊPES WITH RASPBERRY SAUCE

PONTCHARTRAIN

8 crêpes · Pastry cream** · ½ cup raspberry jelly · ½ stick butter · 2 ounces Madeira wine*

Fill crêpes with pastry cream, roll, place on silver platter, and heat 5 minutes in a 350° oven. Combine jelly, butter, and wine, cook until thick, pour over crêpes, and serve.
Serves 4.

* See recipe for crêpes in Crêpes Soufflé.
** See recipe for pastry cream in Crêpes Maison.

CRÊPES MAISON

PONTCHARTRAIN

*8 crêpes**

PASTRY CREAM: *½ cup milk · ½ cup breakfast (light) cream · ¼ cup sugar · ½ vanilla bean · ½ stick butter · ⅛ cup flour*

SAUCE: *3 egg yolks · ¼ cup sugar · 1 teaspoon cornstarch · 1 teaspoon mace · ½ cup breakfast (light) cream · 1 cup milk · 2 ounces rum*

Place crêpes on flat surface and fill centers with pastry cream, to be made as follows. Put milk, cream, sugar, and vanilla bean in a saucepan and scald. In another saucepan melt butter, add flour, and blend until smooth. Remove vanilla bean from milk-cream mixture and add gradually to flour-butter mixture, stirring with a wire whisk. When well blended, let cool. When cool, fill crêpes, roll, and place on a silver platter.
To make sauce: Combine egg yolks, sugar, and cornstarch and beat until smooth. Add mace, cream, and milk and stir to mix well. Cook over hot water until thick, stir in rum, and pour over warm, filled crêpes.
Serves 4.

* See recipe for crêpes in Crêpes Soufflé.

CRÊPES COMMANDER'S

CRÊPES: *⅛ cup flour · 1 egg · ½ cup milk · Pinch salt · Shortening or corn oil*

FILLING: *Grated rind of 1 orange · Grated rind of 1 lemon · ½ pound Philadelphia cream cheese · ¼ cup sour cream · 1 heaping tablespoon sugar*

SAUCE: *½ stick butter · ½ pint frozen strawberries with juice · 1 ounce Grand Marnier · 2 ounces brandy · Powdered sugar*

To make crêpes: Mix ingredients together well and pour a thin layer of the resulting batter into a small skillet that has been greased lightly with shortening or corn oil. Shake pan to prevent sticking or burning. When golden, flip to cook other side. Keep the finished crêpes warm and soft between folds of a napkin until ready to fill.

Mix filling ingredients to consistency of a thick spread. Spoon about 2 tablespoons on center of each crêpe, roll, and tuck ends under so filling does not spill out. Leftover filling will keep in the refrigerator several days.

Melt butter in a chafing dish and add filled crêpes. Add strawberries and juice and heat about 2 minutes. Add Grand Marnier, stir well, and baste crêpes. Warm brandy, sprinkle over crêpes, ignite, and flame about 1 minute. Serve, sprinkled with powdered sugar, on warm plates.
Serves 2.

CRÊPES MARQUISES

ARNAUD'S

2 crêpes · 4 prunes · Sugar · 1 ounce brandy

Make crêpes according to any of the preceding recipes—Crêpes Suzettes, Crêpes Soufflé, or Crêpes Commander's. Place 2 prunes on each crêpe, roll, and sprinkle with sugar. Run under the broiler, then flame with brandy in a chafing dish.
Serves 1.

FRENCH PANCAKES À LA GELÉE

ANTOINE'S

½ cup sifted flour · 1 egg · 1 egg yolk · ⅛ teaspoon salt · 5 tablespoons milk · 3 tablespoons currant or red raspberry jelly · Powdered sugar

Combine flour, egg, egg yolk, salt, and milk. Beat with a rotary beater until smooth, adding more milk if necessary to give the batter the consistency of light cream. Cover and chill ½ hour in refrigerator. Heat a heavy iron skillet and wipe out with waxed paper that has been dipped in melted butter. Pour in enough batter barely to cover the bottom of the skillet, tipping while adding batter. Brown the pancakes on both sides, remove from the skillet, spread with jelly, and roll up. Sprinkle with powdered sugar and glaze under broiler. Serve at once.
Makes about 12 5-inch pancakes.

BEIGNETS

MASSON'S

1 stick butter · 1 cup water · 2 teaspoons sugar · 1 cup flour · 2 eggs · 1 egg yolk · Confectioners' sugar

In a heavy-bottomed pot, bring to a boil the butter, water, and sugar. Add flour all at once and stir vigorously over fire until mixture leaves the sides of the pot. Place mixture in a bowl and cool slightly. Add eggs and egg yolk one at a time and beat thoroughly after each addition. Spoon mixture (size of small egg) in 375° fat and fry until brown. Sprinkle with confectioner's sugar.
Makes about 24 beignets.

POT DE CRÈME CHOCOLAT

PONTCHARTRAIN

1 quart breakfast (light) cream · 6 ounces German sweet chocolate · 2 squares unsweetened chocolate · 1 dozen egg yolks · 1 teaspoon vanilla · Pinch salt

Bring cream to a boil and add melted chocolate. Remove from heat and stir in beaten egg yolks (at room temperature). Add vanilla and salt, strain into custard cups, and chill 4–5 hours.
Serves 12.

POT DE CRÈME À LA VANILLE

PONTCHARTRAIN

2 cups cream · 1 (1″) vanilla stick · ½ cup sugar · 6 egg yolks

Scald cream with vanilla and sugar. Remove from heat and cool slightly. Beat egg yolks until they are light and lemon-colored and add the cream, stirring constantly. Strain through a fine sieve into custard cups. Set the cups in a pan of water, cover the pan, and bake at 325° about 15 minutes, or until a knife inserted in the center comes out clean. Chill.
Serves 6.

SABAYON

MASSON'S

6 eggs, separated · ¾ cup sugar · ¾ cup cream sherry · ¾ cup heavy cream, whipped · 1 teaspoon vanilla

Beat egg yolks with sugar until creamy. Add sherry and cook in a double boiler until thick. Cool in a bowl 10–15 minutes. Add whipped cream and vanilla. Fold in stiffly beaten egg whites. Divide into 4 small ramekins and chill 2–3 hours.
Serves 4.

GRAND MARNIER SOUFFLÉ

MASSON'S

1½ cups milk · 4 egg yolks · ½ cup and 1 tablespoon sugar ¼ cup and 1 teaspoon flour · 4 ounces Grand Marnier · 6 egg whites

Heat milk to the boiling point. Whip egg yolks and sugar together until foamy. Blend in flour, stir in hot milk, and cook until

thickened. Remove from fire and stir in Grand Marnier. Fold in stiffly beaten egg whites and pour into a 6-inch soufflé dish which has been buttered and sugared. Bake 30–35 minutes at 350°.
Serves 6.

OMELETTE AU RHUM

ANTOINE'S

4 eggs · 3 tablespoons butter · Pinch of salt · 2 tablespoons granulated sugar · ½ cup rum

Make a regular omelet cooked in butter. Keep it soft and add pinch of salt and 1 tablespoon of sugar. Turn omelet onto a hot plate and sprinkle the top with remaining tablespoon of sugar. Pass under broiler to caramelize sugar.
Heat the rum, pour it over omelet and ignite. Spoon burning rum over omelet and when fire goes out, serve immediately.
Serves 2.

PINEAPPLE AND LOUISIANA YAMS FLAMBÉE À LA GERMAINE

ARNAUD'S

6 yams · 12 pineapple slices · ⅔ cup flour · ⅓ cup milk · ½ cup butter · 12 maraschino cherries · ½ cup brown sugar · ½ cup rum · 6 teaspoons sherry

Boil yams until tender, peel, and halve. Roll pineapple and yam halves in flour, then in milk, then in flour again. Fry pineapple and yams in butter until golden brown. Place 2 yam halves for each serving on an ovenproof plate. Top each yam half with a pineapple ring with a cherry in the center. Sprinkle with brown sugar and bake 5 minutes at 400°. Heat the rum, pour it over hot yams and ignite. When flame dies, pour 1 teaspoon sherry over each serving.
Serves 6.

SWEET POTATO BRÛLÉ

PONTCHARTRAIN

2 pounds sweet potatoes · ¼ pound butter · Salt and pepper · 12 chopped macaroons · ¼ pound chopped pecans · 1 cup molasses · 2 ounces rum

Boil sweet potatoes, peel, mash, and add butter and seasoning to taste. Place in a casserole and mix in chopped macaroons and pecans. Spread lightly with molasses and brown in oven. Pour rum over the top and ignite just before serving. (Can be made in individual balls.)
Serves 6.

BANANAS FOSTER

BRENNAN'S

1 tablespoon butter · 2 tablespoons brown sugar · 1 ripe banana, peeled and sliced lengthwise · Dash cinnamon · ½ ounce banana liqueur · 1 ounce white rum

Melt butter in a chafing dish. Add brown sugar and blend well. Add banana and sauté. Sprinkle with cinnamon. Pour over banana liqueur and rum and ignite, basting banana with flaming liquid. Serve when flame dies out.
Serves 1.

PEACH FLAMBÊE, MARY MARGARET MCBRIDE

ARNAUD'S

1 scoop vanilla ice cream · 2 macaroons · 2 peach halves · 1 lump sugar · 1 ounce rum

Place ice cream in a dish. Crush macaroons and sprinkle over ice cream. Dice peach halves and put in a chafing dish with lump of sugar and rum. Ignite and flame. While burning, pour over ice cream.
Serves 1.

APPLE PIE FLAMBÉE À LA MAGDELENE

ARNAUD'S

2 scoops vanilla ice cream · 2 slices warm apple pie · 2 ounces rum · 1 clove · Dash cinnamon

Place a scoop of ice cream on top of each slice of apple pie. Ignite rum in a chafing dish with clove and cinnamon. When flaming, pour over pie and ice cream and serve.
Serves 2.

ECLAIR EUGÈNE

BRENNAN'S

½ ounce white crème de menthe · 1 ounce brandy · ½ ounce bitter chocolate · 1 teaspoon vanilla · 1 tablespoon heavy cream · 2 heaping tablespoons confectioners' sugar · 1 pastry shell · 2 scoops vanilla ice cream

Place a deep chafing dish over flame and warm crème de menthe and brandy. Add chocolate, vanilla, cream, and sugar. When chocolate is nearly melted, ignite the mixture in the chafing dish and stir constantly, while flaming, to blend. Just as flame dies, spoon sauce over pastry shell filled with ice cream. Serve immediately.
Serves 1.

COCONUT SNOWBALL

COMMANDER'S

1 meringue · 1 scoop vanilla ice cream · Chocolate sauce · Shredded coconut · 1 maraschino cherry

Fill meringue with ice cream and cover with chocolate sauce. Sprinkle with shredded coconut and top with cherry.
Serves 1.

VOLCANO

COMMANDER'S

1 scoop vanilla ice cream · 1 ounce Cherry Heering · 1 Bing cherry · 2 ounces dry ice · 4 ounces warm water

Put ice cream in the top of a Supreme dish, pour over Cherry Heering, and top with cherry. In the lower section of the Supreme dish, under the ice cream, place the dry ice. Immediately before serving, pour warm water over dry ice, which will cause it to smoke dramatically as the ice cream is brought to the table.
Serves 1.

MAMMY'S DELIGHT

COMMANDER'S

1 scoop vanilla ice cream · ⅓ ounce cream · ⅓ ounce white crème de cacao · ⅓ ounce green crème de menthe · Toasted shredded coconut · 1 maraschino cherry

Put ice cream in a champagne or stem glass. Shake cream, crème de cacao, and crème de menthe together well to make a Grasshopper. Pour over ice cream and top with toasted shredded coconut and a cherry.
Serves 1.

PRINCESS CUP

GALATOIRE'S

1 tablespoon canned fruit cocktail · 1 scoop vanilla ice cream · 1 cherry · 1 ounce orange cointreau

Put fruit cocktail in a dessert glass or dish. Top fruit with ice cream, and ice cream with a cherry. Pour orange cointreau over and serve.
Serves 1.

MILE HIGH ICE CREAM PIE

PONTCHARTRAIN

CRUST: *1½ cups sifted flour · ½ teaspoon salt · ½ cup shortening · 4–5 tablespoons cold water*

PIE: *1 pint vanilla ice cream · 1 pint chocolate ice cream · 8 egg whites · ½ teaspoon vanilla · ¼ teaspoon cream of tartar · ½ cup sugar*

To make crust: Sift together flour and salt. Cut in shortening until pieces are the size of small peas. Sprinkle 1 tablespoon cold water over flour mixture and gently toss with fork. Repeat until all is moistened. Form into a ball with fingers and roll out to ⅛-inch thickness on lightly floured surface. Fit loosely into a 9-inch piepan, pricking well. Bake 10–12 minutes at 450°. Cool.

Layer ice cream in pie shell. Beat egg whites with vanilla and cream of tartar until soft peaks form. Gradually add sugar, beating until stiff and glossy and sugar is dissolved. Spread meringue over ice cream to edges of pastry. Broil 30 seconds to 1 minute to brown meringue. Freeze at least several hours. Drizzle chocolate sauce over each serving.
Serves 8–12.

CHOCOLATE SAUCE

PONTCHARTRAIN

2 squares German sweet chocolate · 2 squares bitter chocolate · ¼ pint cream · ½ cup sugar

Cook all ingredients in a double boiler until thick, using only half of cream to start with. Add the balance of cream to achieve pouring consistency.
Serves 5.

LEMON ICEBOX PIE

PONTCHARTRAIN

1 can sweetened condensed milk · ½ cup lemon juice · Grated rind of 1 lemon · 2 eggs, separated · 1 (8-inch) baked pie shell · 2 tablespoons sugar

Blend condensed milk, lemon juice, grated lemon rind, and egg yolks. Pour into cooled baked pie shell.
Beat egg whites until foamy. Add sugar gradually, beating until stiff but not dry. Cover filling with meringue and bake at 350° for 10 minutes, or until brown. Chill.
Serves 6–8.

Drinks

CAFÉ BRÛLOT DIABOLIQUE

ANTOINE'S

1 (1-inch) stick cinnamon · 8 whole cloves · Peel of 1 lemon, cut thin · 3 lumps sugar · 3 jiggers brandy · 3 cups strong black coffee

In a *brûlot* bowl or chafing dish, place the cinnamon, cloves, lemon peel, and sugar. Put brandy into a ladle, ignite, and pour over ingredients in bowl. Keep ladling brandy over ingredients until sugar is dissolved. Gradually add coffee and continue ladling mixture until the flames fade. Serve immediately.
Makes 8 demitasse or *brûlot* cups.

CAFÉ BRÛLOT

BRENNAN'S

1 (4-inch) cinnamon stick · 12 whole cloves · Peel of 2 oranges, cut in thin slivers · Peel of 2 lemons, cut in thin slivers · 6 lumps sugar · 8 ounces brandy · 2 ounces curaçao · 1 quart strong black coffee

In a *brûlot* bowl or chafing dish, mash cinnamon, cloves, orange and lemon peel, and sugar lumps with a ladle. Add brandy and curaçao and stir together. Carefully ignite brandy and mix until sugar is dissolved. Gradually add black coffee and continue mixing until flame dies out. Serve in demitasse or *brûlot* cups.
Serves 10–12.

ORANGE BRÛLOT

BRENNAN'S

1 thin-skin orange, washed and dried and plunged into hot water 5 minutes · 1½ ounces cognac · 1 lump sugar

With a sharp pointed knife, cut through peel only around the circumference of the orange. Insert the edge of a thin spoon between the skin and pulp, working around entire orange. Carefully roll the skin up from the pulp, turning it inside out with the upper half forming a cup and the lower half a stand for the orange. Fill the cup with the cognac. Put sugar in a teaspoon filled with cognac and ignite. When sugar begins to color, gently float onto the surface of cognac in the orange cup. When the flame flickers, blow out and serve.

RAMOS GIN FIZZ

ROOSEVELT'S

1 bar spoon powdered sugar · 3 dashes orange flower water · ½ ounce fresh-squeezed lemon juice · ¼ ounce fresh-squeezed lime juice · ½ ounce white of egg · 1 ounce Old Tom Gin · 2¼ ounces milk

Fill a cocktail shaker ⅓ full of ice cubes. Add the ingredients in the order listed above. Cover and shake thoroughly to mix and blend all ingredients into a creamy and foamy smoothness. Strain into a tall glass and serve.

SAZERAC COCKTAIL

ROOSEVELT'S

1 lump sugar · 1 dash Angostura bitters · 2 dashes Peychaud bitters · 1¼ ounces straight rye whiskey (90 proof) · 3 dashes absinthe · Twist of lemon peel

To mix a Sazerac requires 2 Old Fashioned glasses. One is filled with ice and allowed to chill. In the other put sugar with just enough water to moisten, then crush with bar spoon or muddler. Add Angostura and Peychaud bitters, rye, and ice cubes and stir to mix and chill. Empty the ice from the first glass, dash in the absinthe, twirl to thoroughly coat inside of glass, and discard excess. Strain whiskey-bitters mixture into absinthe-coated glass, twist lemon peel over drink, and add. Serve without ice.

OJEN COCKTAIL

BRENNAN'S

3 dashes Peychaud bitters · 1½ ounces Ojen

Shake ingredients thoroughly and strain into 3-ounce chilled cocktail glass.

PIRATE'S DREAM

BRENNAN'S

Fresh green mint · ½ ounce grendadine · 1 ounce Bacardi rum · 1 ounce Myer's rum · 1 ounce Christopher Columbus rum · 1 ounce Ronrico 151 Proof rum · Juice of 1 orange · Juice of 1 lemon · 2 dashes Angostura bitters · 8–10 cherries · Orange and lemon slices

In a large glass capable of holding 26–28 ounces, crush a couple of sprigs of mint. Add grenadine, rum, orange and lemon juice, and bitters. Make sure that the mint is well blended into the other ingredients. Fill the glass with crushed ice, adding cherries so they will be spaced throughout the drink. Add cherries to the top of the drink, and a slice of orange and a slice of lemon to decorate the rim. Serve with 8–10 straws.

HALF AND HALF

BRENNAN'S

1½ ounces dry vermouth · 1½ ounces sweet vermouth · Lemon peel

Put dry and sweet vermouth in an Old Fashioned glass with 2 ice cubes. Stir gently and serve with twist of lemon peel.

MILK PUNCH

BRENNAN'S

1¼ ounces bourbon or brandy · 3 ounces breakfast (light) cream or milk · 1 teaspoon superfine powdered sugar · 1 dash vanilla · Nutmeg

Shake thoroughly bourbon or brandy, cream, sugar, and vanilla, strain into an 8-ounce highball glass, and top with nutmeg.

MINT JULEP

BRENNAN'S

2 ounces bourbon · 4 sprigs fresh mint · ½ ounce simple syrup

Put ingredients into a tall 14-ounce glass or silver mug. Fill with shaved ice and agitate with a mixing spoon until the outside of the glass or mug is coated with frost. Garnish with a generous bouquet of mint, orange slice, and cherry. Serve with short straws, so that bouquet of mint will be appreciated while sipping.

ABSINTHE FRAPPÉ

BRENNAN'S

1 ounce absinthe · 2 dashes anisette or simple syrup · Soda or water

Fill an 8-ounce highball glass with shaved ice and add absinthe and anisette or syrup. Add water or soda slowly, agitating ice and liquid until frost appears on the outside of the glass.

ABSINTHE SUISSESSE

BRENNAN'S

1¼ ounces absinthe · 1 egg white · 1 ounce cream · ½ ounce Orgeat syrup · 4 ounces shaved ice

Blend about 5 seconds in a blender and pour into a chilled Old Fashioned glass.

CHABLIS CASSIS

BRENNAN'S

4 ounces Chablis · ½ teaspoon crème de cassis · Lemon peel

Pour cold Chablis into a 5-ounce saucer champagne glass. Add crème de cassis. Stir gently and add a twist of lemon peel.

AMBROSIA

ARNAUD'S

1 dash lemon juice · 1 ounce applejack brandy · 1 ounce brandy · ½ ounce cointreau · Champagne

Shake lemon juice, brandies, and cointreau with ice and strain into a champagne glass. Top with champagne.

BEAUTY AND THE BEAST

ARNAUD'S

1 jigger vodka · 2 dashes lemon juice · 1 jigger crème de cassis · ½ teaspoon grenadine

Shake all ingredients with ice and strain into a martini glass.

GERMAINE SPECIAL

ARNAUD'S

2 dashes orange juice · 1 ounce gin · ½ ounce bourbon · ½ ounce Triple Sec · Champagne

Shake orange juice, gin, bourbon, and Triple Sec with ice and strain into a champagne glass. Top with champagne.

ARNAUD'S SPECIAL

ARNAUD'S

1 dash Peychaud bitters · 1 dash Angostura bitters · 1½ ounces bourbon · 1½ dashes absinthe · Lemon peel

Stir all ingredients over ice and serve in an Old Fashioned glass with a twist of lemon peel.

WINDSOR COCKTAIL

ARNAUD'S

2 dashes lemon juice · 1 ounce applejack brandy · 1 dash cointreau · Sparkling Burgundy

Shake lemon juice, brandy, and cointreau with ice, strain into a champagne glass, and top with sparkling Burgundy.

FRENCH 75

ARNAUD'S

Dash lemon juice · 1 ounce gin · ½ ounce cointreau · Champagne · Lemon peel

Shake lemon juice, gin, and cointreau with ice, strain into a champagne glass, and top with champagne and a twist of lemon peel.

SPARKLE JUBILEE

ARNAUD'S

2 dashes orange juice · ½ ounce vodka · ½ ounce rum · 1 dash Triple Sec · 1 dash grenadine · Sparkling Burgundy

Shake orange juice, vodka, rum, Triple Sec, and grenadine with ice, strain into a champagne glass, and top with sparkling Burgundy.

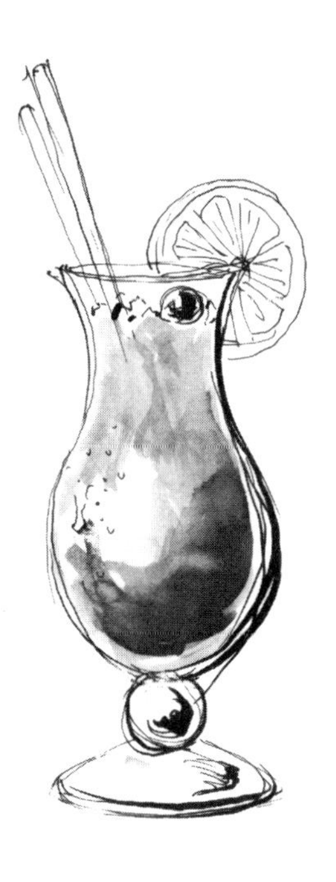

HURRICANE

PAT O'BRIEN'S

2 ounces Jero's Red Passion Fruit Cocktail Mix · 2 ounces fresh lemon juice · 4 ounces dark rum (Amber) · 1 orange slice · 1 maraschino cherry

Fill a hurricane glass with crushed ice, add Cocktail Mix, lemon juice, and rum, and decorate with orange slice and cherry.

SHILLELAGH

PAT O'BRIEN'S

4 ounces white rum · 2 ounces green crème de menthe · 1 ounce sweetened lime juice · 1 ounce lemon-lime Kool Aid · Green cherry · Green stick candy

Pour all ingredients into a blender filled with snow ice and blend. Serve in a 22-ounce white-Burgundy glass decorated with green straws, green cherry, and green stick candy.

SQUALL

PAT O'BRIEN'S

1 ounce Jero's Green Passion Fruit Cocktail Mix · 1 ounce fresh lemon juice · 2 ounces light rum (Carta Blanca) · 1 orange slice · 1 maraschino cherry

Fill a hurricane glass with crushed ice, add Cocktail Mix, lemon juice, and rum, and decorate with orange slice and cherry.

BREEZE

PAT O'BRIEN'S

1 ounce rum · ½ ounce lemon juice · ½ ounce Jero's Red Passion Fruit Cocktail Mix · 1 orange slice · 1 maraschino cherry

Serve rum, lemon juice, and Cocktail Mix in 8-ounce glass filled with crushed ice and garnished with orange slice and cherry.

CYCLONE

PAT O'BRIEN'S

2 ounces vodka · 1 ounce lemon juice · 1 ounce Jero's Gold Passion Fruit Cocktail Mix · 1 orange slice · 1 maraschino cherry

Serve vodka, lemon juice, and Cocktail Mix in an 18-ounce brandy snifter filled with crushed ice and garnished with orange slice and cherry.

LIGHTNING

PAT O'BRIEN'S

2 ounces vodka · 1 ounce orange juice · 1 ounce pineapple juice · Claret or Burgundy · 1 orange slice · 1 maraschino cherry

Mix vodka, orange juice, and pineapple juice in a pilsner glass filled with crushed ice, top with wine, and garnish with orange slice and cherry.

T.N.T.

PAT O'BRIEN'S

2 ounces vodka · 1 ounce cranberry juice · 1 ounce pineapple juice · 1 orange slice · 1 maraschino cherry

Shake vodka and juices together and serve over crushed ice in an 8-ounce glass, garnished with orange slice and cherry.

PURPLE PEOPLE EATER

PAT O'BRIEN'S

2 ounces vodka · 2 ounces grape juice · 1 orange slice · 1 maraschino cherry

Serve vodka and grape juice in a 12-ounce glass filled with crushed ice and garnished with orange slice and cherry.

DIRECTORY

Antoine's – 713 St. Louis Street, 529–5696

Arnaud's – 801–825 Bienville Street, 523–5433

Brennan's – 417 Royal Street, 525–9711

Broussard's – 819 Conti Street, 523–4800

Commander's Palace – 1403 Washington Avenue, 891–5733

Corrine Dunbar's – 1617 St. Charles Avenue, 525–2957

Elmwood Plantation – 5400 River Road, 733–6862

Four Seasons Pastry – 505 Royal Street, 524–5801

Galatoire's – 209 Bourbon Street, 525–2021

Manale's – 1838 Napoleon Avenue, 895–4877

Masson's Beach House – 7200 Pontchartrain Boulevard, 288–9941

Maylie's – 1009 Poydras Street, 525–9547

Moran's – 725 Iberville Street, 523–4664

Morning Call-Coffee – French Market, 523–9841

Mosca's – Waggaman Lane, 776–8942

Old Europe – 631 Bourbon Street, 525–5012

Pat O'Brien's Bar – 718 St. Peter Street, 525–4823

Pittari's – 4200 South Claiborne Avenue, 891–2801

Pontchartrain Hotel – 2301 St. Charles Avenue, 524–0581

Sazerac Bar – Roosevelt Hotel – University Place, 529–7111

Sclafani's – 1315 North Causeway Boulevard, 525–9547

Tortorici's – 441 Royal Street, 523–9567

Tujaque's – 823 Decatur Street, 523–9462

Turci's – 914 Poydras Street, 525–2934

Index

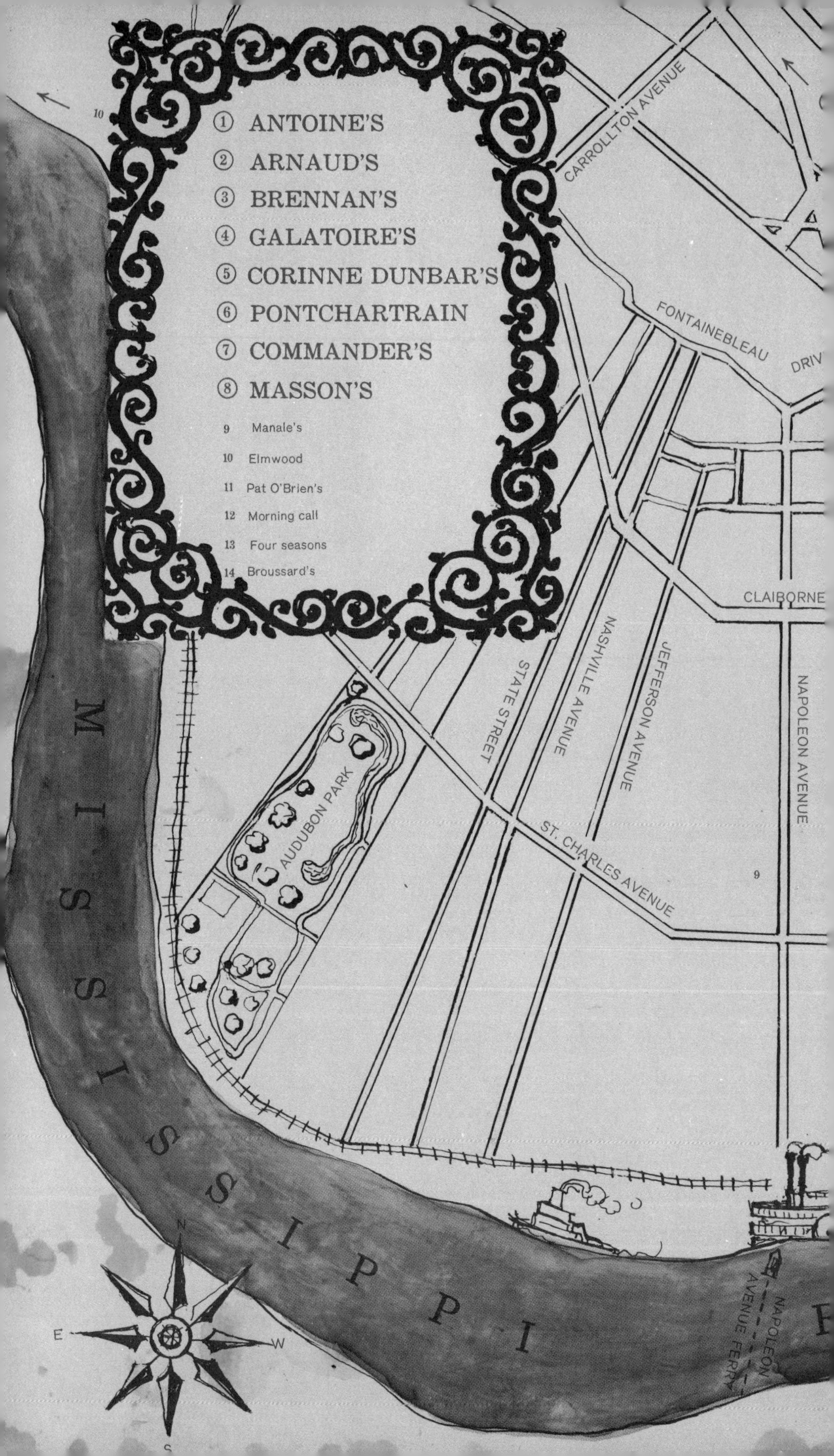

① ANTOINE'S
② ARNAUD'S
③ BRENNAN'S
④ GALATOIRE'S
⑤ CORINNE DUNBAR'S
⑥ PONTCHARTRAIN
⑦ COMMANDER'S
⑧ MASSON'S
9 Manale's
10 Elmwood
11 Pat O'Brien's
12 Morning call
13 Four seasons
14 Broussard's
10
9
CARROLLTON AVENUE
FONTAINEBLEAU DRIV
CLAIBORNE
STATE STREET
NASHVILLE AVENUE
JEFFERSON AVENUE
NAPOLEON AVENUE
ST. CHARLES AVENUE
AUDUBON PARK
MISSISSIPPI
NAPOLEON AVENUE FERRY
N
E
W
S